A
MARCH
OF
TIME

by

ETHEL KILGOUR

To my Generation,
who endured so much for Peace

AaEll
902393

ISBN 0 946920 13 3

Project Editor: Michael Thomson
Project Co-ordinator: Jim Pratt

INTRODUCTION

In my previous book, 'A Time Of Our Lives', I described my childhood in the St Clements area of Fittie during the period when the so-called 'roaring twenties' gave place to the 'hungry thirties', a decade of poverty and unemployment, haunted by the every-growing likelihood of a second devastating war with Germany. Adolf Hitler's intentions for the world had been plain even before he took power in 1933, and by 1935 the threat that he posed was being taken seriously in Britain. In 1937 Germany and Mussolini's Italy bombed Spanish cities as the Spanish Civil War raged – a conflict which we in this country were to realise made a convenient testing ground for the Fascist powers, with their territorial ambitions. The sense of menace was not at all alleviated by the uninvited presence, at the 1937 Royal Naval Coronation Review, of the Graf Spee, one of Germany's latest warships, scrutinising Britain's ageing Naval units and noting their lack of numbers. 'Brittania rule the waves' .....?

Deepening doubts over sustained peace could no longer be ignored. The laying of ships' keels began again in dockyards long empty, and men unemployed for most of the decade found themselves reusing the skills that had been dormant for so long. The building of ships for the Navy and for the sadly decrepit Merchant fleet became a race against time as Der Führer's hysterical rhetoric mesmerised the German nation and events in Europe made ever grimmer reading.

Finally, the Nazi threat became a reality, and we entered on six harrowing years during which nobody knew whether or not Britain might be invaded, whether our friends and loved ones serving in the armed forces would ever come back, or indeed whether after the next German bombing raid they would have anything to come back to.

War is not glorious; it is terrible and brutal, scarring many of its survivors mentally and physically, and wrecking the lives of those bereaved by it. But this was a just war, and we fought it because we had no alternative.

These are my impressions of what the war years and the period leading up to them were like for me and for my family – an ordinary Aberdeen family on the 'home front' during the greatest international upheaval of the twentieth century.

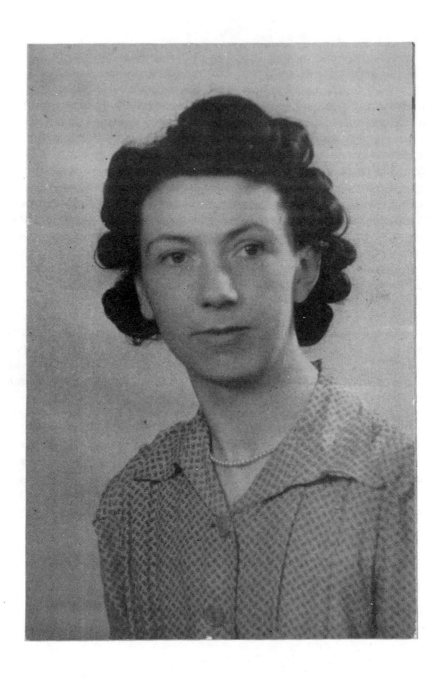

Myself, early war years

CHAPTER 1

I ended *A Time Of Our Lives* with our family's departure from St Clements after losing home and belongings in a disastrous fire at our Church Street flat. We put the cause of the fire down to a dislodged gas poker setting light to a nursery fireguard with clothes on it; those clothes and nappies belonged to my little sister Eleanor, who was born in May 1936. I left school and began work at Messrs Edmond and Spark's printing and book binding works in Queen Street during the following month, and it was for that firm's staff dance, during the autumn social season, that my father bought me my first evening dress. A few weeks later, I planned to go to a Joiners' Dance, but our house caught fire only a matter of hours before it and I lost not only that dress but everything else as well. At an interval of nearly 60 years, dates become less easy to pinpoint, but it was certainly in the autumn of 1936, not 1938, that our enforced move took place.

After the fire, life changed drastically for us. The family spent six weeks living with relatives, while I lived with our great friend Mary Jane Smith in St Clement Street. I had no winter clothes, and Mary Jane very kindly gave me a warm coat to wear on the cold dark mornings when the Edmond and Spark staff had to wait outside on the pavement for the foreman to let them in.

Eventually we obtained a new abode, a recently-built flat at Woodside, where we saw in the year 1937. So alien did we feel that we may as well have been immigrants in another country. We were strangers in our 'spleet new hoose', as my mother called it. The Woodside folk were as close-knit as those in Fittie had been, and were no doubt as attached to it as we had been to our old area, but we missed all the familiar shops and people.

There were compensations, however. For the first time, we had a bathroom with hot water. We revelled in this, realising that because neither Fittie nor St Clements were in the slum category (there was much good quality housing there, superior to many other areas in the city) we would never have had a new house at all but for the fire. Not that my brother James drew much consolation from that. He longed to be back in the maritime atmosphere of his old abode, and at his old school in St Clements. No longer did we hear the roar of the sea on winter nights when the gales blew against our bedroom window. The beach and the harbour now seemed a very long way off, with the lovely sands that had been our playground for so long only accessible by dint of two tramcar journeys and the consequent expenditure of precious pennies.

Over 1937 it was a case of simply setting ourselves up again as best we could. I continued at my job in Queen Street, taking rather badly to the expense of travelling there and back by tram each day. The course of things, however, was interrupted after the summer when I contracted a bout of the then very prevalent scarlet fever, which put me in the City Fever Hospital for three weeks. At first I was quite ill, but thanks to serums and expert nursing I was soon able to enjoy some reading time. My reading material consisted of *True Romances* and other magazines of that ilk, dear to the heart of a youngster of fifteen but the cause of some amusement among the nursing staff, to whom I was just a kid. (In the late 1930s such magazines were considered suited to the more mature.) In the ward was a portable wind-up gramophone, and of the few records that we had to play on it, one, *September In the Rain*, was played so often that I could never hear the song afterwards without thinking of my time in hospital. *September In the Rain* was a very appropriate title, as I heard it through most of that September!

Visitors could not be allowed into wards full of people with contagious diseases, so at visiting time the beds would be moved nearer the open windows. By standing on wooden steps provided (as described in *A Time Of Our Lives*) visitors could communicate with the patients. Any food, fruit, sweets, magazines or comics had to be handed to the Sister in charge at the door. They would be distributed later among the patients, many of whom were children. Eventually the time came for me to return home. I donned my Sunday-best coat, which came in for some admiration from the poorly-paid younger nurses, little knowing for how many more months this nice fashionable garment would have to serve as my 'best'. Time off from work meant no wages at all, and to add to this misfortune my father had taken a bad fall in the fish room aboard his ship, with the result that for a short time he had been unable to carry out his trade as trawlerman.

The winter of 1937 to 1938 was a cold one. Our new house had only one coal fire for heating, but no such things as central heating or double glazing existed in those days, and nobody thought anything about it. Electric blankets were far in the future, and hot water bottles of the rubber or stone 'piggy' varieties did service as bed-warmers. It would be very many years before central heating did become general, and although such things as electric fires, paraffin heaters and (eventually) bottled gas heaters became available, we certainly could never have afforded any of these in the 1930s.

Woodside was in some ways quite similar to Fittie, especially in respect of the many small shops that operated there. It was not necessary to go into the city centre to find a butcher, a baker or a local branch of the 'Copie'. Regular Friday expeditions were, however, undertaken for 'a walk roon' the Castler' – the Castlegate second-hand market. Favourite haunt of Aberdonians, the market was so large that an hour or more was required for a proper 'rakie roon', which would reveal all sorts of treasures from bric-a-brac to tools, clothing and shoes, all of good quality and consisting mainly of cast-offs from the big houses in the West end of the city. It was a place where one could meet up with old neighbours, relations and friends, all having a good browse. These days there are charity and Salvation Army shops to take unwanted goods, but some hint of the old atmosphere survives at the car boot sales which have become popular of late, and which can make an enjoyable outing on a fine day!

We would move on from the Castlegate to the thronged Friday market in the 'Greenie' for dairy goods fresh from the farms, and from there usually to Woolworths, either the 'Big Woolies' in Union Street or the 'Little Woolies' in George Street. Being all on one floor, the George Street Woolies was very popular – so much so that prams had to be left inside the shop near the doors, and often babies could be seen snugly tucked up while their mothers browsed among the multitude of goods on the counters. The size of the crowds meant strict adherence to that rule – can anyone imagine it now?

Undaunted by the distance or the length of the tram ride, which she quite enjoyed, my grandmother made the trip from her house in Links Street as often as she could to help us on washing days. She would marvel at our large, deep white sink and the instant supply of hot water from our zinc gas boiler in the corner of the scullery (some call it 'kitchen' now!). One day in early 1938 she arrived with a piece of news for me – I was being offered a new job. A young woman who lived at the top of Links Street had mentioned to her one day in the St Clements Street 'Copie' that she was looking for a girl to work beside her in an oatcake bakery in Catherine Street. The wage was 12s. 6d. per week (62 pence!), and as I was at that time receiving only 8s. (40p) I was urged to take up the offer. Furthermore, Catherine Street was nearer to my new home, and cycling there would be easy. It was all downhill on Great Northern Road, past the Astoria Cinema and down Causewayend at 'Split The Win'', its junction with George Street. Catherine Street is one of the side streets off George Street, on to which one side of the factory backed.

So it was that I began employment at Lockhart's Oatcake Bakery. On my first Monday morning I found the atmosphere pleasant, friendly and free from the many restrictions to which I had been subject at Queen Street. There were only three employees plus a sales representative, a nice, gentle man whom we saw only at intervals – usually he would be out promoting the company's excellent product. The boss was the lady from Links Street. Named Nessie Allan, her job was to stand at a long table, rolling out the mealy dough mixture, then, by means of a large circular metal cutter with a handle on the top, neatly turning out four triangular oatcakes at a time. These were deftly slid to one side then stacked by Nan Lamont, who took them over to three large hotplates, each of which took 50 raw oatcakes. With a quick wrist movement, Nan would deposit each one until the plate was full, then at just the right moment would turn them over to cook on both sides. Process completed, she would skilfully remove them and stack them on long trays to cool. My job was then to pack the finished product, first in packets of five and then into deep round tins which were finally sealed with a covering label printed with the name of the firm.

I was fortunate enough to be able to sit on a stool – the heat in the bakery was very tiring and made my feet ache. Nevertheless, it was a happy place in which to work, and in Nan I found a new chum. Nessie was what we thought of as 'an older woman' – maybe of 25 or so. Nan and I were only 16, so young and full of enthusiasm for the activities that were dear to the hearts of girls who had to make their meagre pocket money spread out over the week until the next pay day. Nessie was slim and dark-haired, with a pale complexion. Left at home after her brothers and sisters married, she was among the many who had the rather unenviable task of looking after elderly parents. In poor health, they required considerable attention, and during the day (in the neighbourly way of the time), neighbours would 'look in', attending to the fire and making cups of tea.

It was customary for workers to go home at dinner time, which in our case was from midday to 1.15 p.m. 'A rin roon' the table' was the popular term for this. Nessie would take the tram part of the way to Links Street. I would cycle home to Woodside, but as the journey was uphill most of the way and I felt drained after the heat of the bakery, the attraction of this quickly palled. Eventually, I managed to wheedle from my mother enough money to go by tram, although it was made clear that there would be an effect on my pocket-money. 'The carries' were a great mode of transport and very cheap, having a minimum fare of only a halfpenny. There were plenty of stops along George Street or Union Street, and people would 'tram hop' as a matter of course. When the tram came to the downward slope at Kittybrewster, leading to the Clifton Road junction and the Astoria, the feeling was almost like being on the scenic railway as the car lurched, bounced and swayed before rounding the curve and arriving at the stop. I think the drivers quite enjoyed this part of the journey too.

Nan lived in the Froghall area, in a house similar to ours, except that she and her family lived on an upper storey while we lived on the ground floor. Tall and dark-haired, Nan was a nice looking girl with an easy-going nature and an enviable singing voice which was well suited to the blues, at which she was rather good. Nessie also sang – she was a soprano, and although we called her songs 'high falutin' stuff', they were still good to listen to, and this impromptu 'music while you work' lightened the job and made the day pass more quickly.

Nan's background was very like my own – eldest daughter in a large family, so that many of the household chores fell to her, as they did to me. There was nothing unusual about that, and I do not believe that it did us any harm, although we complained about it at the time. We did not, of course, have the labour-saving devices that are taken for granted now, not even a vacuum cleaner. Neither had we such things as fitted carpets, but what we never had we never missed. Most houses smelt of soap and wax polish; I remember the tins of solid floor and furniture polish such as Mansion and Nairns, and the high gloss and clean smell after the application of these plus plenty of elbow grease.

All this time, the Third Reich's sabre-rattling was becoming louder and louder, and the threat of war in Europe ever more frightening. In March 1938 Austria gave in to Hitler's threats. Nazi troops crossed its borders and from then on Austria was completely dominated by Germany. Britain remained outwardly passive while busily preparing for the worst. The building of ships and planes and the manufacture of munitions put back to work thousand upon thousand of the unemployed of the Depression years, but a breathing space was required to allow a country that had become so depleted of everything to regain its manufacturing strength and produce enough weapons to deal with any eventuality. So the policy of appeasement was followed as Britain desperately strove to make ready for what it hoped might never happen.

At the Bakery, we had other things to think about – for example, what colour of evening dress Nan should choose for that year's Dee Swimming Club Ball which we were to attend at the Beach Ballroom. As we worked away at our oatcakes, our conversation consisted of practically nothing but this all-important event. I already owned a long dress (pale orange in colour and at 30 shillings from Parkinson's in George Street, an expensive item) with a pair of silver dancing shoes to accompany it. It was late in the social season, and sales of evening wear were plentiful in George Street, our favourite shopping area. The 'in' colour of 1938 was a sort of lilac blue described as 'amethyst'; Nan and I went to a small store in George Street and she bought a dress in that shade. It had an overlay of net and she was thrilled to bits with it – her first long dress. (It may also have been the only one that she bought for a very long time!)

The big night arrived. Like most girls of our age, we were good dancers, having had plenty of practice at the ninepenny or shilling dances in the city's many halls. The Beach Ballroom was a great venue for the bigger occasions, with its sprung floor and central fountain surrounded by flowers. The floor was always so thronged that there would have been no room for the tables that are set around it nowadays. The band was excellent, and its tempo perfect.

In the large circular Ballroom, the standard conventions were observed – girls on one side and boys on the other, every girl hoping that she would not end up a 'wallflower'. Even as the busy tramcars laden with people intent on a good night out were still arriving at the doors, the first number began. It was preceded by a crowd of young men fastening the jackets of their best suits as they crossed the floor to invite the girls to dance. Nan and I were lucky in that we knew quite a number of the lads, so we hardly missed a dance even though we tried to avoid those fellows that we knew were not so adept on their feet. Upstairs in the gallery, soft drinks and coffee were on sale, and the supper consisted of dainty little sandwiches served with coffee in the restaurant – all for half a crown! Home in the tram at 1.30 a.m., tired but happy. It was great to be young.

Back at work, we kept a cat in the bakery, a female, and a fussy one at that. She would eat only fresh fish, and every day I was sent out for 'a fish for the cattie', costing twopence or so at a small fish shop at the George Street end of Catherine Street. The young assistant would wrap it up for me in a sheet of newspaper, we would exchange a word or so of small-talk, and back I would go. A mother of two, she was very pleasant, and I enjoyed chatting with her. In the course of my daily visits we became quite friendly, and she told me that she lived in the Bedford Road area. Her husband was a soldier, and, typically, she worked each morning to eke out his meager wage.

Nan and I shared a lot in common, and we had a lot of fun. Nessie too had something of a social life with her chums from Fittie, Bella and Mollie McGregor. On Monday mornings there was always plenty to chat about as we worked away, taking turns at the mixing. This was done in a special deep-sided tub which could hold a large batch of dough. Rich roast beef fat (delivered in large tins), meal and other ingredients were weighed out on scales and mixed and moulded by hand. It was a case of being literally up to the elbows in one's work, and the heat did not make the job any more comfortable. However, come Saturday at midday we were free for the weekend, and there would be dancing at St Katherine's Club or a visit to the pictures – usually the cheapest seats at the Astoria, the Grand Central (the 'Grandie') or the City Cinema. On Sundays, after a lie-in (great not to have to get up early for work!) I would board a tram to Fraser Place (cost - 1 penny) and walk through to Froghall to call on Nan, who would usually be just finishing some household chore. 'I'll only be a mintie', she would say as she completed some job like the washing of the bathroom floor. Unlike myself, Nan had no sister of an age to help with the housework, so she had a lot to do. My own sister Margaret was three years younger than I and still at school, but she had to take a turn at washing dishes, despite loud protests that she had school work to do. A studious girl, she had passed the exam for admission to Central School, which was the forerunner of the present Hazlehead Academy, and was situated in Schoolhill. Grandmother, after whom she was named, was so proud of her that she bought her a Burberry coat and other items of school wear.

Nan, as I have said, was from a large family – a happy lot, and not too badly off, as her father worked as a linesman for the G.P.O. and her elder brother Joe also brought in a wage. There was of course no such thing as Family Allowance, and the breadwinner's wages had to go a long way. The poverty of the Depression was receding as, ironically, rearmament brought about a revival in the economy, but wages were still very small. Nan's father was head of the house, and was in the habit (not uncommon among the men of his generation) of going for a drink or two on a Saturday night and coming home a little inebriated. I suppose that in view of his having spent a busy week working long hours these excursions were not too much frowned upon.

Formally dressed in best coat and hat, Nan and I would take a Sunday stroll, sometimes meeting other girls at Queen Victoria's statue on St Nicholas Street for a walk on 'the mat'. Then in the evening, back at Nan's house amid a family of small children, her mother, who loved whist, would endeavour to teach us the game. All would go well for a while, but then there would come the exasperated cry of 'Ye gype, ye've reneged again!', the cause of Mrs Lamont's loss of patience being my constant failure to play a clear round.

Mrs Lamont had a good, loving family, and held particular affection for her eldest son Joe. He was tall (like Nan), dark and good looking, about 18 years of age and possessing the mild nature of his mother. He would never be embarrassed when, at the end of the evening, she told him, 'Joe, walk up to the Astoria with Ethel'. This he would do, chatting all the way from Fraser Place until we reached the tram stop by Clifton Road, from where the journey home cost only a halfpenny. He would talk enthusiastically about his work as a steward on the railway. His duties took him from Aberdeen Joint Station to Elgin and Lossiemouth, and he had many amusing stories to tell. One day Nan and I went with him on one of his working trips, spending a few hours in these two towns and picnicking on sandwiches which we brought, together with a flask of tea. It was most enjoyable, and I thought Joe looked so handsome in his uniform. Perhaps my liking for Joe became apparent to his observant mother, as it was certainly with a little matchmaking in mind that she instructed him to walk me to the Astoria, but to be truthful I had no wish for a 'lad' (the expression of the time for a boyfriend). I preferred my chum's company, and if Joe was really interested in me or in any other girl, he never mentioned it. His work and family were always the topic of his conversation, although he was never boring. We never spoke about the possibility of war, but Joe, like so many young men, was very soon to be wearing a uniform of another kind.

It is worth noting here that in those days seeing someone home like this was a friendly and gentlemanly gesture, not a matter of protection, although romantically-minded young girls rather liked the idea of having an escort, and didn't mind rewarding him with a little kiss for his trouble! The question of safety never seemed to arise when making our way home at night, and certainly I cannot remember ever being afraid to walk in the dark streets when the necessity arose. Compared with the situation nowadays, young girls of our generation were extremely lucky.

As 16 year-olds, we girls were much less worldly than our counterparts of today. In fact, we were really very naive about the opposite sex. Girls who were more free with their affections were said to be 'fast', and it was rumoured that 'good men' would never marry them. We preferred each other's company when walking home from the dancing, and any lad who tried to take liberties became known to us through the female grapevine. In these cases, the question 'See you home?' would simply be answered with 'No, I'm ga'n hame wi' my chum'. What 'liberties' were, we were not exactly sure, as most of the boys that we knew socially were 'fine loons'. In my memory, none smoked (not enough money for that) and certainly none drank, as even if they had been able to afford it, none of them had yet reached the age at which they could enter a pub. Pubs were for the more mature man to escape into after a hard week.

Turning to family matters, 1938 was the year in which my sister Nora was born, increasing our numbers to seven. I have to admit that in view of the financial situation at the time I felt quite annoyed at the thought of yet another addition to the family, but on voicing that opinion I received a good telling-off from my mother. My chum Nan was in the same situation, and we commiserated with each other at some length. Of course the babies were lovely, and we adored them, but, naively, we simply could not understand why we had to have yet another mouth to feed. As it was, my brother James went out on a milk round each morning before school to earn a little money with which to supplement the family income.

My grandfather, John Masson, continued to enjoy his Saturday night nip and pint in the St Clements Bar, much to the annoyance of my grandmother, whose grim facial expression of a Saturday night after supper left no-one in doubt of her views on such things. Her disapproval was heeded not a jot by my quiet 'granda', who spent all his week nights at the kitchen table, humming a hymn tune while working on his wonderful model ships. In my younger days I would often watch him shave, slowly and carefully stropping his open razor, which he used with great concentration. When pleased with the result, he would tuck back the collar of his dark working shirt and would wash himself at the kitchen sink. He was always reluctant to take that shirt off, but on Saturdays he was made to don a white one. This was to accompany his best (and only) navy blue serge suit with matching waistcoat and carefully knotted tie. The addition of black socks and polished shoes, white hanky in pocket and best cloth cap completed this once-a-week sartorial ritual, after which he was ready to mingle with the social scene at the St Clement.

This was no doubt paralleled in many other households in those days. The womenfolk, meanwhile, would stay at home or go to the cinema if they could afford it, which those with children rarely could. Pub-going was a male pursuit which as far as women were concerned was not done. Naturally, not every man did go to the pub. For many couples, if they could raise the funds, the most popular evening out was a good film and a bag of sweets – and there were plenty of good films to choose from. The cinema was also a great haven for courting couples. It enabled them to get away from the family, especially if the family was large, the house small, and the front room had already been commandeered – often the case when there were two or three sisters, each of whom had a lad!

Houses were still generally very basic, especially the new council ones into which people were being moved to ease overcrowding. Few folk could afford anything other than essential furnishings like beds, a wardrobe, a sideboard, etc, and the time-honoured linoleum floor covering, with rug or mat at the fireplace. Better quality lino had an inlaid pattern, so that the scrubbing which it received did not make it fade into a drab brown, as with the cheaper varieties. Most floors were well polished, which entailed a great deal of hard work.

Our new abode was particularly spartan thanks to the fire at Church Street, from which the only thing saved was a dining table, rubbed down, restained in oak and reused. The insurance payment had been so whittled down by deductions for 'wear and tear', gas meter, electricity meter, etc, that we ended up with very little money with which to make a new start. However, the good quality lino had been bought and gradually the house was being made to look like home, especially after my mother bought in the Castlegate Market some nice cretonne curtains with plenty of width for our large windows. They were expertly adjusted to fit, and the left-over pieces provided cushion covers. The whole family had to be reclothed, and as money was so short everything had to be well looked after. When my grandfather eventually retired, he and my grandmother moved to a single apartment in the Masson family house in North Square, Fittie. Even after a lifetime as ship's carpenter and (as far as I remember) never a day off work through illness, there was no golden handshake for him, only a poor state pension. Economics had to prevail, and so my grandparents gave up their home in Links Street, taking with them only what they really needed, including their lovely mahogany ogee chest of drawers which I mentioned in *A Time Of Our Lives*. We fell heir to a small oak dressing chest and one or two other items, and the remainder was divided among the other members of the family. But all the woodworking tools (and there were lots of them) went to Fittie, where, in the shed, Granda resumed his model-making activities, beginning with another little fishing boat!

Aberdeen is fortunate in having its two rivers and its beautiful parks as places for relaxation on a fine day. In the spring of 1938, once the cold of the long North East winter had given place to warmer days, the Lamont family decided to have a Sunday outing – a picnic by the Don. I was invited, and we all boarded a tramcar to the area at the mouth of the river. Each of us carried a bag of eatables, a towel or two, and a blanket to sit on. We found a nice spot in the dunes by the water's edge. The tide was turning, which was lucky as there were potholes in the deeper areas which made swimming unsafe at high tide. We spent a lovely day wading in the water and eating our sandwiches in the sunshine. accompanied by entreaties from Mrs Lamont to the younger children to 'Come oot o' the dubs – ye'll get intae a sotter!'. There were some places in which, unlike the nice clean beach, the sand was dark and muddy looking, probably because of the paper works close by. We all returned home happily sunburned; simple pleasures, but life was sweeter for them.

As I have already mentioned, the bakery's working week finished at 12 noon on Saturdays, so that Nan and I were free until Monday morning, but that same spring we heard that the very busy 'Little Woolies' in George Street required Saturday girls. Off we went to see the Staff Supervisor, and we were taken on. After a test in addition and subtraction in pounds, shillings and pence, we were shown how to give change correctly. This instruction stood me in good stead; nowadays, cash registers are so sophisticated that the operator has very little to do. Not so then!

Our Saturday employment at Woolworths began at 1.30 p.m. After finishing at the bakery I would hurry home in the tramcar, take a quick bath (luxury!), and have a cup of tea and a sandwich before hurrying off again. The bath, I should explain, was necessary because the smell of oatmeal from the bakery clung to our clothes and skin, and became all-pervading. For the same reason, Friday nights became hair-shampoo nights. The steel curlers that we used were the bane of our lives, demanding very careful unwinding, otherwise the process could be rather painful. At the best of times, the end result tended to be rather frizzy with broken ends, due to the curlers' design. Later, when 'Dinky' curlers appeared, much of this hair-tugging discomfort was eliminated.

At Woolworths on our first day, we and and our fellow young hopefuls were each provided with a standard plum-coloured dress with full zipped front and a collar with a large letter W in gold thread on either lapel. In order to encourage honesty, it had no pocket. The lady supervisor stood with us while we deposited coats and handbags in the cloakroom, which was then locked. We were allocated our various counters and, feeling very nervous, were ushered down to the shop floor, with instructions given on the way as to tea-break times. I was to work in Stationery, with two older girl regulars. This counter had two cash registers, and soon I was working 'all out' in a mêlée of ringing till bells and voices demanding service in the crush of Saturday afternoon shoppers. The store closed with the sound of clanging bells at 9 p.m., then stock had to be carried up from the basement. That was the work of the Saturday staff, and heavy work it was too, but we enjoyed all the excitement and bustle, and of course it meant the handsome and welcome addition of 5 shillings a week to our pocket money. With our remaining energy, we walked the mat or went dancing.

The girls in the shop were friendly, and we made some new chums with whom we could share our leisure time. Many of the older staff were engaged, and I remember one telling me that she and her fiancé were saving up £1 a week. She proudly showed me her engagement ring, which was very pretty and cost £7 – a lot of money then. Most of the younger engaged girls set great store by what went into their 'bottom drawer' as they gathered what they could for their future home and marriage. They would speak of embroidering supper cloths and the like, all very romantic, but to we 16 year olds it was all a bit staid. We had no thoughts about steady lads; we enjoyed the company of the boys at dancing, but as none of them had any money to pay us into the pictures we didn't have dates to separate us from our chums!

I had, however, once been a bridesmaid. This exciting occasion was the wedding of one of my two young uncles with whom I had been brought up in Links Street. Andrew and Georgie had been my constant companions in my younger years, having been obliged to take me with them to the 'Starrie' or to the Duthie Park to sail the little boats and yachts made for them by my Granda Masson. Andrew had finished his apprenticeship as plater at Hall Russell's shipyard, and, emerging as a fully fledged journeyman, had married his fiancée Nellie just after I left school. The brief wedding ceremony was held in the Rev. Robertson's manse at St Clements. The bride was in blue, and I wore the long pale orange dress that I had bought for special dances and other occasions. I wore a silver half-tiara on my head, while on my feet I wore my silver dance shoes. We both carried enormous bouquets of flowers. The bridegroom and his best man (a pal from the shipyard) wore their best navy-blue serge suits with carnation buttonhole, and each sported a liberal application of Brylcreem to ensure that not a hair was out of place! The wedding meal was held at my grandmother's house in Links Street.

No such ties were in sight for Georgie, who, only five years older than myself, remained unattached, enjoying life as he walked the mat with his pals, dressed in his fashionable black coat and white silk scarf, and no doubt keeping an eye on the girls there. Georgie had a lot of friends, and I would meet them from time to time at my Grandmother's house. Some of them, like Georgie, were in the 'Terriers' – the Territorial Army. Sometimes on a Sunday, Nan and I, in company with one or two of the other Woolies Saturday girls, would take a tram ride to Hazlehead Park. The 'carries' then ran straight from the Castlegate to the park gates, the last part of the journey being along an avenue made specially for the tram lines. This lovely park was very popular as a result of that easy access – a facility now no longer available, as the public transport entrance track is long closed, and for those who do not own a car a longish walk is now involved! Sundays, being the only work-free day of the week for us, were enjoyed in all manner of ways, especially when the weather was fine. As the augmentation of my income through working at Woolies allowed me to continue taking the tram to work at the bakery, my bike was now used for pleasure only – Sunday trips to places like Collieston and Stonehaven, and to smaller villages not too far from home. On these outings I was accompanied by a friend named Betty Selbie, who lived in the same street as myself. Dressed in matching shorts and jackets (we even had a snapshot taken of ourselves in this smart and fashionable attire) we would revel in our freedom after being cooped up indoors all week. Where we found the energy for this I don't know – not only had we been working during the previous day, but we had been out dancing at night!

We paid weekly visits to the pictures, and found that if we queued at the side door of the City Cinema in George Street we could get into the cheaper front seats for 4d. Sometimes a seat in the 'gods' at the Tivoli Theatre would be preferred, and many a good variety show we saw there for only a few pence. Aberdeen was a good city for the young person in 1938. The sophistication of the present day was lacking, but our expectations were different. There were plenty of pursuits for those who were prepared to go in search of fun and recreation, and not all cost money. If all our funds had been spent, which quite often they had, there was always a walk to the beach or around a park at the price of only a little shoe leather. Occasionally, four or more of us would visit the Uptown Baths for a Sunday morning swim, not for any serious sport but just 'for a laugh'. At St Katherine's Club, where we sometimes attended the Saturday night dances, there began a weeknight keep-fit class, which we joined. For this, we wore sleeveless, knee-length outfits of pale blue cotton, with matching knickers. Thin and loose, with splits down the sides, these gave the coolness which was essential during a couple of hours of what is now referred to as aerobics, and which gave rise to much moaning and groan-

16

ing as muscles that we never knew we had were persuaded to carry us upstairs on the tramcar home! In those days anti-perspirants and deodorants were not on the market, and we used lots of Woolies' cheap cologne and lavender water, of which a large bottle cost only 6d. It was not so easy for anyone to keep 'B.O.' at bay, but such things were not deemed as important as they are now.

One day I went with my Aunt Daisy to George Street to buy a new dress for dancing. This may seem hardly worth remarking on, but at that time few girls owned more than two or three dresses, and the purchase of a new one was definitely an occasion. In one of the many fashion shops in George Street, I chose a pretty brown dress trimmed with brighter colours and with the puff sleeves which were then very much in favour. Made of crêpe material, it cost 8s. 11d. – 45p now, which seems incredible, but it still meant a big sacrifice to my mother's purse. It was duly taken home and fitted with arm pads to stop any staining from underarm perspiration. These pads were sold in packs of two, and were made of cotton on one side and thin rubber on the other. In the absence of modern materials, great care was required at the laundering stage in case garments shrank, a disaster which could not be remedied.

Underwear was separated into what we wore for work and what we wore as our 'best' at weekends. Work gear consisted usually of Celanese (artificial silk) knickers with elastic at the knee. Favoured by all ages, these were available in thicker material, and could be drawn over stocking tops in winter. For weekend wear, or for the occasional weeknight trip to the dancing, a briefer type of underwear was worn. Elastic was sold by the yard in most shops, including Woolworths, and constituted a most essential commodity. Old elastic would perish and finally snap, with potentially embarrasing results, especially when underwear slid floorward, which it would invariably do at the worst possible moment. Elastic was also used to make garters for keeping the artificial silk stockings of the time from wrinkling. A pair of real silk stockings, with back seams and shaped heels a darker shade than the rest of the garment, were a joy to wear. They were the very essence of luxury, and very becoming to the wearer, but at 1s. 11d. or 2s. 11d. from Reid and Pearson's they were reserved strictly for dancing!

CHAPTER 2

My way of life was now radically different from what it had been during my Fittie childhood. Neither I nor any other members of the family would have wished to go back to the kind of poky old house that we had shared in Links Street, but I looked back fondly on my happy, carefree days as a rather spoilt child for whom father's return from the sea meant dress circle seats at the Tivoli, coloured comics, patent leather shoes for school, etc, and that delicious ice cream from 'Lookie' – all now just a memory, along with the Saturday 'tuppenny rush' with my schoolboy uncles at the Starrie. Of course I now had many other pursuits of the kind that appealed to my age group, but wages were still small, our family was larger and treats did not come so easily.

In the average family of 1938 Father was still the patriarch – the breadwinner, while Mother was the mainstay of family life. My own mother was still a young woman of 35, and had remained slim and youthful despite having had seven children. Responsibility for everything pertaining to the running of the household was placed firmly on her shoulders – washing, cooking, cleaning, looking after the children, ensuring the payment of rent and other domestic bills, and providing new clothes when necessary, in all of which she (like many others) worked miracles. The mother of that era demanded and usually received respect from her family. Any infringement of rules would incur her wrath in no uncertain fashion. No 'ifs or buts'; the question 'Are you wantin' a lickin'?' would be followed by a good slap on the backside. My father was still frequently away at sea for a couple of weeks or so at a time. On his return he would take my mother out to the pictures, but amusements were fewer.

Neither my father nor my brother cared for the new house – 'Too far away from the Fish Market', my father would say, and my brother was no happier at his new school. It was a cold house, and due to transport costs (or so it was claimed) coal was very expensive in the North East, with the result that we could not afford large quantities of it to make fires. We usually ordered it from the 'Copie' or from Messrs Ellis and McHardy, and it was delivered straight to the house. Often wooden 'cloggies' would be bought to help eke out the coal supply. These would be delivered by a man with a horse and cart. No doubt sawn up in some cold wet wood out in the country, they were usually very damp and required drying out, but they were none the less popular in the city as an economy measure. Houses then were all much the same, and would continue to be so for many years more. My own children were brought up in a very similar one.

18

Despite what might nowadays be seen as privations, we were a healthy lot. Our usual medicines were syrup of figs for constipation and Granny's poultices for just about everything else. A bad cold would be treated with hot gruel and aspirin, the gruel consisting of oatmeal and milk (quite nice to drink – we didn't mind taking that!), and sometimes also a teaspoonful of whisky for the more adult invalids. It was a good cure for colds. To aid recovery after an illness, my mother had her own preparation, a switched-up mixture of egg, sugar and warm milk, which we found very comforting. At approximately 3s. a visit, doctors' bills were a thing to be avoided, but when the doctor did have to be called, he usually prescribed M and B tablets. Preparations using penicillin had yet to appear, although this discovery by the Scot, Alexander Fleming, was to play a great part in the saving of lives during the world conflict that was to come.

At home, Friday nights were busy ones. They were house-cleaning nights, and no amount of pleading or cajoling would persuade my mother to release me for social activities. To the strains of the latest popular tunes on the wireless, we would scrub and polish away, thankful that at least we no longer had old-fashioned brass rods or candlesticks to clean. The only brass that we had to deal with was the taps in the kitchen and bathroom, which if left unattended would start to go green with verdigris. My sister Margaret and I would have heated arguments about who did what, her excuse being school homework, which on a Friday night was ignored. I would remind her that I had done well at school despite having chores to do, but sadly no evidence of my academic success could be produced, as all of my school prizes, comprising six books, had perished in the fire at Church Street together with the certificates for my RNLI and League of Nations essays. I also lost a fine embroidery sampler completed at Frederick Street School under the guidance of the arts teacher Miss Wright, who, to my surprise, declared it excellent. Framed and hung on the wall, it too was gone.

The wireless was a great boon in those days before television. At night, Radio Luxembourg was a favourite station, playing the latest tunes by the big bands of the time. Before the fire, we had owned an Ekco set; I remember its large circular case of handsome, shiny bakelite. The earlier ones were, I believe, made of wood – my grandmother had one of these, but mostly they were manufactured in the other cheaper material. Those 'wireless sets', as we always called them ('radio' is a much more recent term), were large and heavy, with a solid metal chassis and a complex of glass valves inside. It took the needs of war to trigger research into miniaturisation. Music-to-work-by-made our Friday nights much more pleasurable. The three boys in the family did small chores, but like most of their peers were allowed to go and play football on the road outside. It was on those same streets that later a boy named Denis Law was to first kick a ball.

My aunt Daisy, her husband Andy and their two children had by this time moved to a top flat in a rather posh tenement in Victoria Road, Torry, and I was a frequent visitor there. I usually brought a chum with me, and we were made very welcome. Daisy was young and outgoing, always ready to listen to tales of lads, dancing and who I was going with to the pictures. During the summer Trades Holiday – a whole week away from work! – we planned to go as often as money would allow to the Beach Ballroom, where dancing sessions were held each afternoon over the week. It was also the time of Glasgow Fair, to which we looked forward because we reckoned the Glasgow boys to be very good dancers. Daisy showed me some lovely silk dresses with brightly coloured hand embroidery. These had been sent to her from the Philipines where Andy's sister lived. Married to an 'ex-pat' Aberdonian, Daisy's sister-in-law and their family of two little girls lived in the luxury that colonials then enjoyed abroad. For the week, she lent me one of the dresses, which, as we were of the same height and build, fitted me nicely. It was of white silk, and I felt very elegant in it. The Glasgow lads' dancing came well up to our expectations, and the lads themselves were full of good humour and Glasgow patter. One, who worked for a dairy company, came home to the door with me, but my father was home from sea and I had to be in at the allotted time or else! However, I did go to the pictures with him before he went home.

Holiday week or not, it was work as usual at Woolies that Saturday, then back to the bakery on the Monday, and so the summer of 1938 went on. One rather important thing occurred – I at last became proficient in the game of whist as taught to me by the ever-patient Mrs Lamont. Card playing was then a very popular Sunday evening pastime. Families would visit each other to sit endlessly playing after Sunday tea. It was an important part of the social scene, and as visiting was done on a regular basis it made easy the keeping intact of family life. Usually the system was that each family took a turn at providing hospitality – a case of 'Cheerio then, oor hoose next Sunday'. I remember how our old house in Church Street was a refuge for Andrew and his pals, three unattached lads, who would turn up dressed in their Sunday best after being out and about, no doubt walking the mat. Of a dull Sunday evening they would adjourn to our house for tea, biscuits and a game of cards, usually playing for matches as they had no money left. The Masson house would have been no place to go and play cards under any circumstances – Grandmother would have been quick to send them on their way, just as she had done when the drums and chanters appeared!

Most shops were closed on Sundays, as were all places of entertainment, so young people had to rely on themselves to find amusement. Even in the rough weather of February and March, when the sea was stormy, people could be seen walking along the North Pier or the Prom, taking the air and watching ships, especially trawlers, as they battled their way out to sea or homewards over the bar where the fresh water of the Dee met the salt water of the North Sea. Often trawlers would seem to disappear completely into the troughs before bobbing up again, rather to the relief of the watchers. Even as teenagers we would have fun running up and down the steps leading to the water, where at high tide and with a rough sea the waves would splash wildly in a wide arc over the bottom step. Anyone doing this had to be quick and agile to avoid a soaking or worse; not the safest of pastimes, but to us it was great sport.

The beach and the sea have always, as will have been gathered, held a fascination for me, be the weather calm or rough. I still never tire of them, but then anyone brought up on their margins as we were would share that feeling. Nowadays I prefer to wade or swim in warmer climes than ours; wading at Aberdeen beach is still quite enjoyable, but those balmy days now seem so few and far between.

During the first warm days of that summer I had met up once again with Madge Grant from Fittie. The Grant family, as I recorded in *Times Of Our Lives*, owned a large bakery on the corner of St Clement Street and Lime Street. Since that time, the family had moved to a bungalow with a new bakehouse next door in an area of private housing in South Anderson Drive, and was doing well there. It was great to renew friendship with Madge; she and her chum Alice Watson, myself and my chum of that summer Betty Selbie joined forces and had fun going out as a foursome. One Sunday at the beach we were kicking our beach ball around when some lads thumped it into the water. Indignantly, we demanded that they retrieve it, which they did, and that little incident began a friendship which lasted all through that summer and Autumn, and several weeks into 1939. The lads, four of them, a little older than ourselves, were very good company. I remember the names of two of them, Bill Masson and David Paton. Like ourselves, they had little money to spend, so on week nights we all went 'Dutch' to the pictures and on most Sundays we walked in the park. We would rendezvous 'at the Queen' for our excursions, but (perhaps strange to relate in this day and age) we did not pair off at all – we were all just good friends.

In the course of Saturday work at Woolies, I struck up friendships with a few of the other girls. One of them, Peggy Walker, remained a companion until the conflict of 1939 when she was called up into the forces. We still meet from time to time. Her father, George Walker, was a tram conductor and later worked on the buses up until his retiral. I remember him as a fine, jovial man. Peggy was an only child, and it was a pleasure to escape from our large household on the Sundays when I visited her for tea. Her mother was quiet and reserved, but very welcoming to Peggy's friends.

We never had cards or cakes with which to celebrate birthdays. With the increase in the size of our family, these occasions had become very much less auspicious ones, so invitations to birthday parties came as very welcome entries in the social calendar. Aunt Daisie's children both had the same birthday. She always had a small celebration for them and a few of their chums, and I and one of my friends went along as helpers. Adult parties were more fun, though, especially when 'Postman's Knock' or 'Bottlie' were played in young mixed company. Those kissing games were enjoyed by all, with plenty of the Aberdeen 'ale' in between – in all kinds of fruit flavours!

As we enjoyed that summer in the company of our four male pals, the papers seemed full of news from Germany. In the cinema, the monotonous tones of the British Movietone News announcer were heard over film of Adoph Hitler and his henchmen. It still all seemed so far away from our little island, but there was nevertheless a slight feeling of relief when the 'big picture' came on, especially if it was an American one, American films being the favourites.

The organs of the Astoria and Capitol cinemas were popular, with audiences singing along as the little 'bouncing ball' picked out the words on the screen. Cinemas always seemed to have queues outside them, especially for the cheaper seats, which could cost from 9d. down to as little as 4d. Settling back in warmth and comfort, the men would light cigarettes or pipes, considered a luxury along with the bag of sweets for the ladies and the ice cream during the interval. My parents' favourite was to share a bag of peppermint creams. They loved their visits to the pictures; before going out they would leave us strict instructions to behave. All younger members of the family were to be in bed on time, and there was to be no making of toffee or puff candy. Good organisation was therefore necessary to ensure that all toffee was eaten, utensils washed and put away, the house tidied, and all traces of our nefarious activities erased by the time that my parents returned. Of course we knew discipline at home and in school, and although it was resented at the time I think it did us a power of good. We only ever really disobeyed in our clandestine toffee-making!

As previously mentioned, we only saw my father on the occasions when he was ashore. His job on the trawler still took him away for two and sometimes three weeks at a time, depending on the choice of fishing ground. He never seemed to forget his time in the army as a young man during the first World War – his service in India was a favourite topic of conversation, and he had many interesting stories to tell. My mother was quite the easy-going kind until something or someone made her really angry. We had then to watch out, as a firm smack on the behind or dunt on the shoulder, depending on the age of the offender, could be in the immediate offing. However, she was a good listener to all of our problems, which ranged from requiring help with school homework to my own teenage moans about lack of fancy clothes (or at least that was how it seemed to me – for someone so deprived I always seemed to be very neatly dressed!) My mother did have one strong fixation. She detested seeing anyone with down-at-heel shoes, especially if the person was otherwise well-dressed. One day in town we were making our way towards the Buttery in George Street for our 'fly-cup' when she nudged me and with her eyes directed me to a woman who was dressed in a fur coat but had on her feet a pair of shabby old shoes with worn heels. 'It's like haein' a fur coat an' nae knickers' was the popular expression for such a situation.

As a sixteen year-old, I very much wanted to show off a little when out dancing or when out with my friends on a Sunday, strutting our idea of fashion in our best apparel. One Sunday I was giving full voice to my discontent with my wardrobe; 'I'm fed up with this coat – I've worn it every weekend', and so on. I went into my bedroom, still griping about these highly important matters, and heard the door shut and lock behind me. My mother had had enough! An angry voice shouted through the keyhole, 'Fit div ye wint, jam on it?', one of her stock answers to silly problems. Undaunted, I climbed out of the window, which was at ground level, and went off to keep my rendezvous with my chums. Coming home on the tram later in the evening, I quaked rather at the thought of the reception that might be awaiting me, but all I received was a look that said, 'I'm dying to laugh'. I think she gave me points for ingenuity, as after the warning, 'I'll tell your father when he comes in from sea' the episode ended.

In those days, married women were not considered employable. 'A woman's place is in the home' was the attitude, so young women got married, kept house and usually had a baby within a year of marriage, followed by more. Dole queues had receded to some extent, but were still long in 1938. Young unmarried women filled jobs considered unsuitable for men, wages were meagre, and equal pay for both sexes was still a very long way off. Just as during the worst years of the Depression, young lads who had served their apprenticeships at a very small weekly wage found themselves jobless as soon as their time was out. They were treated as nothing more than a source of cheap labour, although for many who had worked in shipyards or in engineering those 'time served' papers would one day mean a 'reserved occupation' rather than the armed forces.

Agriculture in this country had suffered years of governmental neglect, causing hardship to those who wrested a living from the land. A married couple lucky enough to be employed by a farmer would be given a cottar house (probably very primitive), potatoes, meal and milk in return for a working day that lasted from early morning until dark. In the harsh, bitter North East winter the unrelenting hardness of the ground was made worse by snow and fierce frosts. Single men fee'd to the farmer lived in bothies and slept in the 'chaumers' or chambers therein. The famous 'bothy ballads' originated from this way of life, in which those hardworking people made their own entertainment in the Buchan fashion, and in their own rich Buchan tongue. Now, many young lads, brought up in such an environment and with the only advantage in life the excellent quality of teaching by their local school dominie, were looking beyond the confines of the farm. They were watching their fathers pulling turnips from the frozen ground and deciding to strike out and join the army. The North East's own regiment, the Gordon Highlanders, was full of such men and boys as they exchanged the rigours of Buchan country life for postings to British colonies in India, the far East or Singapore. Hardened by their backgrounds, these 'country loons' took well to the disciplined life, and made fine soldiers in the best tradition of the Gordons.

During our time in Woodside, only two families out of the six in our block really became friendly with us, the Dalgarnos (on the top floor) and the Cruickshanks. Mrs Dalgarno, who I remember as a quiet-spoken dark-haired woman, was a Londoner. She had met her husband while he was in the Guards; now he was unemployed. A tall man, I remember his shabby suit which he always wore with a shirt and tie. I became chums with their daughter Phyllis, with whom I recall cycling to Fyvie Church one Sunday, a trip of 52 miles there and back.

The younger Cruickshanks were all younger than I. Their mother, who had been brought up on a farm, spoke in the Buchan tongue. An affable woman with the dry wit of her kind, she always had stories to tell of her country childhood. Her husband was, I seem to recollect, a joiner who worked in one of the local hospitals, and it was the bane of their lives that he was paid on a monthly rather than a weekly basis. The day before pay-day was always referred to as 'the day before the coo calved'. They were hard up, but cheery all the same. I remember Mrs Cruickshank finding a meal mill somewhere by the River Don, no doubt the Don Mills at Balgownie. With babies in arms, she and my mother walked there and purchased a large threepenny bag of freshly ground meal. We had a fine supply of excellent porridge and skirlie for quite some time after!

With the Autumn of 1938 came another major crisis in the already very tense European situation. The latest subject of Hitler's lust for power was Czechoslovakia, in the Bohemian area of which there lived about 3 million German speaking people to whom Hitler was the saviour who had raised Germany like a phoenix out of the ashes of the first World War's aftermath. The Treaty of Versailles had left Germany a conquered nation paying recompense to France, but Hitler had stopped all that. Now these German-speakers, who had suffered badly in the world depression, wanted to be part of Germany, and Hitler and his Nazis were only too pleased to oblige.

The world paused with bated breath as Britain's Prime Minister, Neville Chamberlain, travelled to Munich to meet Hitler in an effort to strike a compromise and avert a war for which this country was not ready. During the 'Munich crisis', we girls at the Bakery were entertained (for want of a better word) by a man who worked as gaffer in a wholesale warehouse on the other side of the narrow street. A small, excitable, talkative fellow, he came over to tell us that he was putting out large quantities of sugar, tea, etc to folk 'in the big hooses in the West end'. In other words, those who could afford it were stocking up on food in this national emergency. On the September night when, after what seemed like an eternity, Chamberlain arrived back with that piece of paper proclaiming 'peace with honour' and 'peace in our time', this country breathed again. But the truth was that Chamberlain had signed a pact handing over part of Czechoslovakia to the Third Reich. Certainly it was essential to buy time, but on the face of it 1938 was indeed the year of appeasement.

In our school days we had been told very little about the 'Great War', that time of appalling carnage to very little end. Two decades on, people who had suffered themselves or had lost loved ones thought it inconceivable that the same thing could happen again, but when, earlier that month, Chamberlain made his first trip to see Hitler, war seemed so inevitable that the Navy had been mobilised and the organisation of Civil Defence begun. Now the sense of relief was enormous. My grandmother cut out the newspaper photo of Chamberlain waving his piece of paper, and, like so many others, went to church that Sunday to pray for peace.

Not so our little mannie from the warehouse. He appeared next morning, dressed as usual in white apron and shirt sleeves, but dancing with rage instead of joy. He had been inundated with requests to take back the large bags of dry goods that had been delivered at the time of the crisis. His anger was not unjustified, and we commiserated with him, though afterwards we thought it a great laugh. We marvelled at the cheek of some people, but then who knows – if we had been more affluent would we perhaps have filled our own cupboards?

That Christmas we worked as normal, and soon it was Hogmanay. Our four lads, with whom we had passed many Sundays in the summer months, did not care for dancing, so with the advent of winter we did not see so much of them. My friend Nan preferred to spend Hogmanay at home with her family, but our house was often visited by old pals of my uncle Andrew who, although now married and settled down, still kept in touch with them. Georgie brought along some friends from work, so there

25

was no lack of company for me. First footing was always great fun, and was very much looked forward to. Armed with small gifts, we would celebrate in style, although despite the presence of the traditional bottle of whisky or port on the household table along with the cheese, fruitcake and shortbread, none of we younger folk indulged in strong drink. When the first stroke of midnight ushered in the New Year, bottles were opened, health drunk, and 'All the best for 1939' wished with heartfelt sincerity.

As I have previously mentioned, Aunt Daisy's house in Victoria Road always had an open door for me and my chums, especially after the bells at New Year, so after many greetings and a few kisses in town where we younger fry had gathered, off we trekked to Torry. South Market Street was thronged with first-footers, and shouts of 'Happy New Year' rang out as we crossed Victoria Bridge. The atmosphere was jolly, and we sang as we walked along. The newsreel films of Adolf Hitler and his Nazis goose-stepping across the borders of beleaguered countries could not have been further from our minds. We were young, we lived on an island, and we believed our elders when they said that this country could never go through such terrible traumas so soon after the horrors of the Great War.

Daisy's home was filled with young people that night. Uncle Andy, home from sea, gave us a warm welcome and handed everyone a glass of sherry in his own inimitably hearty manner. The fruit cake and cheese were dispensed by Daisy, and so the party began. By the time that we were ready to move on, Andy was just a bittie inebriated and was bellowing out his favourite song, 'Oh, we ain't got a barrel of money', etc, which was his usual party piece at family gatherings or weddings. It was in fact only on such occasions that he ever took a drink – he was otherwise quite teetotal.

'Jist like anither Sunday' was the general comment on New Year's Day, when, energies spent, families sat or lay around lethargically while the womenfolk prepared some dinner. 'Naething like a plate o' Scotch broth t' buck ye up', my mother would say, and she was right. This would be followed by some trifle, which was our usual Sunday pudding. New Year was a holiday from work, unlike Christmas Day, which was celebrated only with a visit to the cinema. Unfortunately, Christmas Day 1938 fell on a Sunday when all cinemas were closed, so it was a dour affair. Oh how Aberdonians loved their pictures – a haven of escapism in a very troubled world. To leave the cold drizzle outside for a couple of hours' worth of warmth, comfort and Hollywood sunshine, even if only on celluloid, was bliss. The old Starrie in Park Street, so fondly remembered from my childhood, was still providing seats (albeit hard wooden ones) in fantasy land for the modest sum of 4d., and people were happily continuing to patronise it.

In winter time, a Scottish Sunday could be a very dreary affair, but if the weather was dry, young people would flock to 'the mat' as usual. There would always be an undercurrent of excitement, perhaps the possibility of seeing some member of the opposite sex from a dance the night before. We would walk along gazing into the shop windows, which, in the case of Union Street shops like Watt and Grant, A.C. Little, Falconer's or 'E and M's' (Esslemont and MacIntosh) was all that we were likely to be able to do. We eyed up with not a little envy the fabulous real fur and fur-collar coats, dresses made of luxurious materials and shoes made of real leather. The fox fur, worn carelessly slung around the shoulders, was admired but not really desired by us – although very fashionable, it was considered more suitable for the older woman.

The 'Big Woolies' in Union Street, with its three floors (one of them a restaurant) usually had in its windows an interesting display of the latest gramophone records which we scrutinised carefully for our favourite tunes until the bobbies moved us on and we rejoined the walkers. I remember Father taking my mother and I to Woolies restaurant for a meal during one of his times on shore during Links Street days.

As a young child, always dressed in the best, I had been extremely fortunate. Now, although the younger children in the family still usually got their comics and a penny or two, things were much more difficult. My father's job as trawler cook was a hard, exacting one, in which he had to keep the crew well fed, and at home he was often critical of the meals put before him. My mother made excellent plain, wholesome food, but with the family income having frequently to last two weeks at a time, and sometimes longer, meals could never be exactly lavish, or even on a par with those aboard ship. However, my father's time ashore was short, and when he went back to sea we ate what the household could afford, which often meant 'serve sma' and serve a''.

At this time, the beginning of 1939, I was the only wage earner in the family apart from my father, although my sister Margaret, being fourteen years of age that September, would then be due to leave school. But that was not until September, and meanwhile I worked on at the bakery during the week and at Woolies on Saturdays, happy with the extra pocket money that the latter gave me to buy stockings and toiletries (from Woolies, of course) when required. Soon winter would pass and with it worries about having to buy coal in quantity. My grandparents, now settled in Fittie village, were fortunate in being able to gather coal and driftwood washed up on the nearby beach and store them in the garden shed for winter. Ships still fired their boilers with coal, and jettisoned residues were always being brought ashore by the tide. Fittie folk never had to worry about having a fire in the grate – the sea was a good provider, and it was the cleanest coal ever!

Significantly, my last visit to my grandparents in their old Links Street

27

house had been on the occasion of my last 'big' dance, in long dress and full evening outfit, at the Beach Ballroom. I was accompanied by my old chum Dorothy Gordon from St Clements Street, and afterwards we walked home at 1.30 in the morning down the prom, she to her house and myself to a 'shakkie doon' on Grandma's kitchen floor. I elected to do this rather than travel all the way to Woodside, as although we never had any fear of walking in the dark, it made sense to have each other's company. The next morning (or should I say later that morning!) I got up from my mattress, packed my finery in a bag, had breakfast and left to go to work as usual. I did not know it at the time, but my next visit to the Beach Ballroom would be a very long time away.

June of 1939 saw the appearance of an exciting new diversion for the young people of Aberdeen – an ice rink. Opened in Spring Garden by the city's 'entertainment kings', the Donald family, it drew crowds of enthusiastic aspiring skaters, including myself. To the strains of 'The Blue Danube', I and a few pals clung to the railing, helplessly inept at this new pastime until, much to my surprise, a boy that I knew from Church Street days came over and, as the waltz played, guided me in a graceful glide around the ice. All went wonderfully until, after a 'thanks, Ethel', the lad over-confidently let me go. I slid into a corner and fell in a heap. The rink was extremely popular, some of its patrons going on to such things as bronze or silver medals in the skating classes that were held there, but nobody that I knew ever attained such heights – it was just too costly for us. Furthermore, there were rumours that because of the many spills and bumps being sustained during skating, being off work now carried the risk of dismissal. Whether this was true or not I do not know, but if so it was a risk that many were happy to take! A large ice stadium was planned by another concern, the Aberdeen Ice Rink Company, for a site on Anderson Drive near the Garthdee housing scheme, but world events soon halted that operation, and Donald's Ice Rink carried on unchallenged for many years.

As the 1939 Trades Holiday week drew near, Aberdeen's popularity with Glaswegians was as apparent as ever. These good-natured, cheery folk arrived at the Joint Station in their usual large numbers, hell-bent on enjoying their Glasgow Fair holiday despite the very ominous rumblings from Europe. They descended upon a mainly stay-at-home city, for, as we asked ourselves, 'who needs to go away when we have a lovely beach and so many facilities for enjoyment?' Of course, no-one could guarantee the weather, and on inclement days shops and cinemas did a roaring trade. This always seemed rather a shame – my mother once exclaimed sympathetically, 'They've a' the shops they need at hame, an' the picters too'! Sunshine package holidays abroad were not even a glimmer in the working class mind of the 1920s or 1930s; a short holiday by the sea anywhere in good old Britain constituted the event of the year for those who could spare the cash. Anyone with a suitable room would take 'holiday fowk' for the week, and my grandparents in their Links Street days would let out their front room, with the stipulation 'Nae quines - they pit their face poother ower a'thing'! After their move to Fittie this was impossible; they had only a single apartment, with Georgie sleeping in an attic bedroom.

On the international front, it was now clear that there would be no more treaties with Hitler, who, tearing up the Munich Agreement, made Czechoslovakia the latest victim in his treacherous quest for territory. Italy, which, for all the strutting, posturing pomposity of Benito Mussolini, was considered very much the lesser Fascist power, had invaded Albania that April, and a growing threat to Poland by Germany had led to a pact, signed that spring, in which Britain and France pledged their support in the event of attack. Rearmament was gaining momentum, recruiting campaigns had begun, and it became known that a policy for general conscription had been laid down by the Government. Already, lads of 20 were being called up to 'the militia', supposedly for a 6 month period of training. Air Raid Precaution (ARP) training also began for volunteers, and the Navy's Reserve Fleet was called up to begin exercises. Hitler, meanwhile, turned his hysterical abuse towards Britain and France, who dared to oppose his dream of power. Britain was still not ready to face the might of Nazi Germany, and time was running out as the prospect of war seemed to loom nearer with every outburst in Der Führer's litany of hate.

Work at the bakery with Nessie and Nan was also approaching a rather crucial point. Tins of oatcakes were piling high in the little stock-room, and production now went on at a rather slower pace. Conversation flowed in the usual easy manner; Nessie had attended the wedding of one of her friends, and we were relayed full details of the church ceremony and reception, enlivening one rather dreary Monday morning. It seemed to us that weddings were becoming more frequent as couples who had prepared for the customary longish engagement threw caution to the winds and, apparently regardless of financial considerations, splashed their slowly-saved money on a shower of happy, confetti-filled wedding parties.

My contribution to that Monday morning's chatter was an account of a visit to the pictures with a male acquaintance who had nearly finished his apprenticeship as a painter and decorator. We both lived in the Woodside area, and so went to our local cinema, the Astoria. During the walk home after an enjoyable show, my enthusiastic companion, whose idea of conversation was apparently to enlighten me on the value of such practical information, gave me a full step-by-step description of how to decorate a house. When I told my mother, she laughed. 'You should hae asked him in – he wid be handy t' ken!' It was nevertheless true that she set great value on lads who had a trade. My three brothers, James, John and Andrew, were still schoolboys, James being only 12 years of age, so there was no immediate anxiety as to their future, but to families with children of the age of Nan and I, times became more worrying and uncertain as the political scene worsened. Our friend Mrs Lamont, for instance, had been very concerned for her son Joe ever since he had mentioned his intention to join the Royal Air Force if and when he was called up. The Lamonts had a large (in fact, ever increasing) family, but to his mother Joe was very special, and a similar situation was to be found in many close family units. My own grandmother lamented the fact that her younger son Georgie was in the Territorial Army, although Georgie, with whom I had been brought up and who was five years my senior, simply shrugged his shoulders and replied in his laconic way, 'It'll maybe nivver happen'.

Meanwhile, Der Führer was caricatured unmercifully in the British press. Jokes about his appearance, especially his rather comical moustache and his exaggerated posturing, provided a source of laughter to many in lighter moments, but a chill ran down the spine when Hitler was heard addressing crowds of Germans, with 'Sieg Heil' ringing out in response. We saw it often enough in the Pathé and Movietone newsreels, those mighty goose-stepping armies that Britain seemed more and more likely to have to face, but then Hitler would never invade Poland – would he? Mrs Cruickshank ('Cruikie'), our very Buchan-spoken neighbour, enjoying a fly-cup and a scone in our house with my mother and granny one afternoon, remarked in the drily humorous way of the North East, 'Fit, nae fancy piece the day ? Jim's surely nae in fae sea yet!' 'Hitler?', she continued, 'Hitler's jist a feel! Losh, if I hid my hands on 'im richt noo he wid be too feart t'fecht onybody!' Spoken with great bravado no doubt, but she concluded by remarking, 'If we didna lach we wid greet', a remark which neatly summed up the philosophy of the times in which we lived.

Summer drew to a close with Sundays, our only free day, given over to pleasurable recreation at the beach. At the end of a working week, it was good to breathe the fresh salty air again while playing, like children, with a ball or wading in the water. We did not swim, as this would have caused too much bother with the tongs in repairing our coiffure. Instead, we protected our hair from the sea breezes with kirby grips (six or so to a card from Woolies), ensuring that waves and curls stayed in place.

For reasons not difficult to guess, there was at that time rather a rush to buy metal goods such as grips and curlers, and also steel wool for cleaning and polishing the latest innovation – aluminium pots and pans. Previous to this, all pans had been enamel lined and were apt to chip, although really good ones could last for many years. Pails, basins, bowls and babies' potties were practically all enamelled, as were chamber pots, which could be found under many a bed in those days when outside toilets were general. Yes, the old 'po' or 'gizunder' was still a necessity in many homes. China ones, bedecked with floral designs, and often with matching water jug and basin, were a bit posh. They could be seen on top of bedroom washstands, some of which were themselves very ornate, with coloured tops and curved legs in marble. Our family had one like this in Church Street, as the sink was on the landing outside and we disliked having to wash there!

In shops, purchases were wrapped in brown paper then tied with string, the assistant usually making a loop for ease of carrying. In Woolworths, every item sold had to be put in a paper bag (no plastic bags in 1939) before it was handed to the customer. There was even a bag size for a single pencil or eraser, ensuring proof that the goods had been paid for.

The lack of a National Health Service and the consequent incurring of doctors' bills for treatment spawned extensive advertising in newspapers and magazines for patent medicines with which to cure ailments of all kinds. Aimed mainly at womenfolk, the products that manufacturers sought to promote included laxative chocolate, syrup of figs and Bile Beans, the latter serving to aid slimming and general fitness as well as curing constipation. An attempt to introduce legislation on family allowances had been thrown out by the Government, and the efforts of Dr Marie Stopes to promote family planning had met with a very cool reception. Many women continued to have large families, with confinements mainly at home rather than in hospital, which cost money. Home births, with no help from the drugs that are now available, were an agonising ordeal; the men, of course, were kept well away and never saw the raw side of giving birth. An oft-heard remark was 'If men had to have the bairns there would be a lot of one-child families'!

One Sunday in late August 1939 I walked with one of my chums along the Prom to Fittie village, enjoying the warm sunshine and the sight of a calm sea. Fittie was always an interesting place, with so many memories of my childhood not so very long before. There, my grandmother (or 'Grunny', in our Aberdeen vernacular) made us as welcome as ever. A cup of tea and a slice of fruitcake (of the kind known as 'slab cake') with a piece of cheese on top was set down for us at the small table. I have heard non-Aberdonians describe this combination as a little peculiar, but to us it was delicious, and a visit to my Aunt Daisy always occasioned the serving of the same things at tea or 'fly cup' time.

In my childhood, the two brothers and the sister on my mother's side of the family were never known as 'Uncle' or 'Aunt' unless some formality was required. They were much more likely to be called 'Oor Andrew', 'Oor Georgie' or 'Oor Daisy', with the grandparents simply known as 'Granda and 'Grunny'. Strangely, however, their counterparts on my fa-

31

ther's side were given their titles, but they came from Central Scotland, where habits were different from ours, and to be honest they could not always understand our Doric speech. Talk of 'loons' and 'quines' caused them quite some amusement, as did our continual use of diminutives, and even more so our habit of doubling or even tripling the diminutive by adding 'little wee'! But then I remember how, on the trip that I made as a little girl with my chum Olive to my Auntie Nan's, a few miles from Glasgow. I thought people there spoke most peculiarly. An ice-cream cone, always a 'cappie' to us, was a 'poky hat', a slider was a 'wafer', a double chocolate slider was a 'black man', and a bag was a 'poke'. The 'copie', so beloved to us in Aberdeen, was 'the Store' or 'the Co', with a system that seemed very slow and alien compared with the speed and effiency (with no 'tick') to which we were accustomed. It was all so different, and it contributed greatly to the homesickness that made us glad to return to Aberdeen and made Aunt Nan vow never to have us again after all our greetin'. 'Hame again', Olive told her mother. 'There wisna even a beach, and they spoke funny!' The train journey, which took us over the Forth Bridge, was all right – we were allowed to throw pennies in the water far below – but Aberdeen Joint Station, with its smell of fish, was very welcome, and the sight of Aberdeen's shining granite was all we needed to recover from our sojourn in foreign territory.

I recollect that my Aunt Nan, the most genial and generous of women, did in fact have me back again on one or two occasions. Once I went with my sister Margaret, and we were taken to 'the Store' on the village's little main street, where Nan bought us each a pair of leather sandals to save our patent leather shoes. It was all very leisurely and friendly, with everyone known to one another, and the shops acting as places where small-town gossip could be relayed and discussed with interest – something to which we were quite used in our own community in Aberdeen. It was very different in the big city shops, where everything was very detached, people were just 'customers' of no identity, and most assistants spoke 'pan loaf'. My thoughts on the subject of Doric are that it must not be allowed to die out. Of course we must remember that people from outwith the North East, and especially from abroad, find the local brogue difficult to pick up, but let the accent remain, modifying words where necessary. People who have lived away from the area have said the same thing to me. Ours is a proud and unique heritage that must be preserved.

CHAPTER 3

On 1 September 1939, Germany attacked Poland. Britain and France sent an ultimatum to Hitler, who ignored it, and on Sunday 3 September at 11.15 a.m. Britain's anxious population heard on the wireless the tired and broken voice of Neville Chamberlain declaring that 'a state of war now exists between Britain and Germany'. As those long-dreaded words came over the air, there was great anger that once again Germany had provoked an international conflict. Furthermore, many considered that Czechoslovakia had been 'sold down the river' by Britain in the interests of appeasement, an action which had now proved futile. It was a bitter time.

I heard the news from my bedroom, where I had been having a 'lie-in' after an unusually busy Saturday at Woolies. My mother shouted to me and turned the volume up so that I could hear the announcement. I thought of the lads that I knew, decent fun-loving boys who had never been away from home. I thought of Georgie, in the Territorial Army, and of Andrew's pal George from the boatie excursions. The unmarried one of two brothers, and a member of Aberdeen Journals' staff, he was a regular visitor to our house.

What might this conflict bring? There was already great fear of the Luftwaffe; air raid sirens had been installed all over the city, and we had heard their wail during ARP practice. That evening the liner Athenia, outward bound for Canada with 1400 people on board, was torpedoed without warning, and there was great loss of life. The war had begun with a vengeance. During that first week, all cinemas and theatres closed for safety reasons, but soon we were back in the queues again. Work continued as usual, but now with a sense of excitement, a feeling of the unknown, which added a new dimension to our little 17 year-old world. We watched the 'Terriers' walk down Union Street in full uniform, kit bags perched on shoulders, on the way to the railway station and from there to goodness knew where in England. After some more brief training, they would be sent to France as part of the BEF. Suddenly the city was full of men in uniform, including ARP (Air Raid Precaution) staff. A complete blackout of all visible lights was decreed at nights, sandbags were piled outside every building, and shops had their doorways blocked with plywood, making a baffle so that no light would escape when the doors were opened. Their windows were similarly covered. The rush was on to buy blackout material for house windows, which were already criss-crossed with tape to stop shards flying if the glass was shattered by blast. Everyone had to carry a hand torch, so torches and batteries had to be purchased, no doubt making the manufacturers very happy, although they too may have had other things on their minds.

The outbreak of war put back to work thousands more men who had been on the 'scrapheap' for years. Factories worked to capacity and beyond, churning out uniforms for the services, boots, gas masks, and all the necessary paraphernalia. Those in 'reserved occupations' – in shipyards, steelworks, coal mines, munition works, etc – worked round the clock in a sustained effort to meet demand, an effort which still fell short of the necessary targets. Meanwhile, only hours into the war, U-boat packs began hunting down British merchant ships as Germany attempted to starve this island country by means of a blockade. Concrete air raid shelters appeared in streets and back gardens everywhere, and smaller garden shelters called Anderson Shelters seemed to take root as they were dug in where flowers or vegetables had once been. Every other bit of garden space, including lawns, was turned over to the growing of food. 'Dig For Victory', said the posters, and this was done with great dedication, as if every spadeful of soil was a blow against Hitler. Initially, the most difficult task was the putting in place of the blackout curtaining on all windows, glass doors, etc. Roller blinds in the permitted colours of black or navy blue were all right for those who could afford such things, but they were expensive, and they still had to be covered over with thick, dark curtains so that not the tiniest chink of light showed in the evening or in the darkness of the night. During daylight hours, window coverings were a major source of irritation, causing hard work and fraying of tempers in every household, including ours. The greater number of windows to deal with, the more the mutterings of 'scunner' and 'damn that bloody Hitler!' Everyone had lessons to learn in the art of blackout, but as the weeks went on and 1940 approached we gradually became conversant with all the 'rules and regs'. Something that we did learn very quickly was to respect the voice of the ARP warden shouting 'Get that out!' when a light showed. Not to obey immediately was to risk a fine.

'Showdie-powdie, pair o' new sheen; Up the Gallowgate, doon the Green' Granda had made a new wooden swing for my two little sisters Eleanor and Nora. Hung on strong, thin rope from steel hooks in a bedroom doorway (most handily the one off the living-room), it gave the youngsters great enjoyment as members of the family passing by gave it a little push to keep them amused and to stop them from getting in the way while the pantomime of sewing tape and hooks on curtains went on. Granda had come up trumps yet again with another well-made wooden toy to add to the many that he had made over the years. He was now hoping to find work of some kind in the shipyards. 'Too auld?', he said, 'Nivver! Div ye ken there's a war on?'.

My father was now a member of the Merchant Navy, though still a trawlerman, and on his return home he showed us his little 'MN' badge. Many large trawlers had been taken over by the Navy for equipping as mine sweepers, but trawl fish constituted an important source of food, so most of the Aberdeen fleet remained untouched, although each boat now sailed with a gun on board. Father seemed to develop a new enthusiasm for his work, which, although dangerous at the best of times, with a constant challenge from the weather, had now been taken out of the mundane by the war. I have no doubt that the gun received maximum spit-and-polish and plenty of greasing in preparation for 'haein' a shottie at the Hun'; with memories of first World War service and the terrible scenes that he had witnessed still fresh in his mind, my father wore that MN badge proudly.

In the midst of all the changes that were taking place around me, and amid talk of ration books and gas masks, points and coupons, I entered on another new phase in my life – a change of job. As we had rather expected, the oatcake bakery began to reduce its output, due, I suppose, to lack of vital ingredients, but fortunately the idleness that I might consequently have faced did not materialise. Back in Church Street days, while still at school, I had helped a downstairs neighbour who made fishing nets at home. This young woman, a Mrs Laing, took up net-making after her marriage, in common with many others whose husbands went to sea. She had no family that I can remember, and I often helped her with housework while she worked at her nets. A great deal of experience was required by these 'braiders', as they were called. Knowledge of each part of a full net ready for sea was essential, as was knowledge of 'how to do the knot' at speed. With a quick movement learned through sheer experience, she filled special wooden needles with trawl twine, and soon she taught me to do this for her, saving her time. She went on to show me the rudiments of net braiding, which stood me in good stead; late in September 1939 I commenced work at Enterprise Trawl Net Stores on Albert Quay.

With this change in work and location came a change in lifestyle and a lot of new people to get to know. Also, because I was on 'piece work', I had the chance of earning a far better wage. On that first Monday morning, I boarded the tram, alighted at St Nicholas Street terminus, then walked down Market Street and along the quays. By this time, a security cordon had been thrown around the whole of the dockland area. The harbour was now filled not only with cargo ships but also with naval vessels, which were anchored in the Albert Basin, under particularly strict security. The whole harbour area was now enclosed by a very high wire mesh fence, with gates manned by a guard who checked every person going in or out. Anyone with business in the area required a security card for admission; card in hand, I was checked in through one of the smaller gates which were placed at intervals along the length and breadth of the docks, so many were the people who required access in order to reach their employment.

Happily, I already knew some of the Fittie girls alongside whom I was to work. Entering the building, I climbed a wooden stair to an L-shaped loft in which I was allocated a net-braiding stand. The foreman or 'gaffer' was a nice quiet-voiced little man named Jimmy. Perched on a high stool at a desk, he wrote on an ordinary school slate the words 'mending net'. I was to 'cast on' 200 loops on a heavy iron bar held across my small work area by sturdy brackets, but first I had to fill my first two dozen or so wooden needles. This done, I had to stand on a clean wooden fish box provided so that I could reach the iron bar. Later, when the net was half completed, I would need the box to sit on (a welcome rest). Personal effects and filled needles were kept in a receptacle rather like a carpenter's tool box, one of which was placed alongside each girl, dividing her work area from the next's. Two or three army-type stoves provided heating in the place, doubling as means by which to boil kettles or heat soup when break time arrived. It was a friendly scene in which laughter and chatter never stopped. Jimmy sat at his desk, sometimes smiling wryly at the conversations around him as he supervised the work and ensured that hands were kept busy. On the occasions when he had to go downstairs to where the riggers worked, I'm sure he was glad to escape for a while. He was said to be a good-living man, and when the Fittie girls and women began singing the hymns that they had learned at the Mission Hall (or 'Schoolie', as it was known) he was pleased to hum the tunes along with them.

The 'Schoolie', to which I referred in *A Time Of Our Lives*, is situated in the centre of the old fishing village of Fittie, and its bell would ring and echo around the houses before each service. 'When the roll is called up yonder I'll be there', the girls would sing; this was a favourite, but there were many others, all sung with the same fervour. Torry was also well represented, and I'm sure that more than half of the workforce came from that other maritime community whose solid granite houses were buffeted by the same winter storms as Fittie. Hardy characters all, reared to live beside the North Sea and to make their livelihood from it in all its varying moods.

'Blisters!', I complained to my mother. 'I can't get them healed at all!' My hands were a sorry sight after a few days of handling that tough, bristly twine. A health visitor who called at the works had applied some soothing cream and had bandaged my hands, but bandaged hands were no use in what I had to do. I was shown the real remedy by the other girls. Each of them kept a bottle of white methylated spirit which they constantly rubbed on their hands to soothe them while also toughening them until some had palms resembling leather. Gradually my hands, hitherto soft and white, took on a much tougher texture, which increased my working speed and consequently my wages!

This did not happen overnight. There was a lot to learn, but soon I was promoted from the mending square to working on other parts of the net – the 'wings', the 'belly', and, hardest of all, the 'cod end', which is the bag part of the net. The making of the cod end was left to the most experienced women as it had to be worked on with the smallest 'spool' (the brass gauge which determined the size of the openings) to give a tiny mesh for this the net's most important area. When the full net was hauled inboard, the cod end would be drawn together and closed with all the fish inside until emptied on to the ship's deck.

With my new workmates, I began a new social life. The war did not deter the folk of Aberdeen from pursuing enjoyment; there was a wider scope than ever in the choice of dance halls, and many excellent films were appearing in the cinemas. In the course of our 'walking the mat', new faces were seen as the uniformed armed forces came to the North East, to be stationed not only in barracks but in drill halls, schools and private billets all over the area. It was all quite exciting. Strangers (in uniform, of course) took the place of 'weel-kent faces' as we danced or we stood in cinema queues. If we wanted to see the whole of the programme at the pictures, we had to go early, as, in the interests of patrons' safety, there was a 10 o'clock curfew so that cinemas would be cleared as darkness fell. We would sit there and sing 'Run, Rabbit Run' or 'We're Gonna Hang Out the Washing On the Siegfried Line' to the music of the Capitol or Astoria organs; the war was to bring many songs of that kind, and anyone who could play the piano at parties was assured of being in demand when the sixpenny song sheets were brought out.

A small group of girls from work arranged to go to an ATS dance at the Abergeldie Ballroom one night. We bought tickets in advance for the event, which I remember was in October 1939 and was the first of its kind held by the military. I borrowed another of my aunt Daisy's dresses, a very pretty one with a printed apple pattern in pale green and yellow. In the hall, where as usual a 'live' band played, there were many newly-conscripted soldiers – 'rookies' in their new army life, who endeavoured manfully to dance fox trots, slow waltzes, etc in their new, stiff army boots ('bulled' to perfection, with a superb shine on the toe cap) without treading too often on their partners' toes. There was also a number of lads in 'civvies' who were apparently still waiting for uniforms, the battle still being on to provide these quickly. One chap in a grey suit danced with me quite often, and during this he informed me that his name was Bill and that he came from a small village (of which I had never heard) in the depths of Lanarkshire. I noticed some of the girls having a cup of tea or lemonade at a NAAFI counter in the hall, and, feeling thirsty, ventured to mention that I fancied a drink. A look of surprise appeared on his face, and he muttered, 'I don't drink'. Swiftly and angrily I answered back, 'Neither do I!', and stalked off to tell the girls. None of us in that circle had the money or inclination to drink or smoke, and I was very annoyed. Next dance was a 'ladies' choice'; I crossed the dance floor and chose as a partner a tall soldier standing next to the gent in grey, who I saw walk out.

This enjoyable evening went on until about 10 o'clock, when suddenly a loud voice was heard, followed by much stamping of feet. The Sergeant Major was inviting his charges to return to barracks, in all the choice verbals that only a Sergeant Major knows how to deliver. We looked on astounded and amused as, with much more stamping of feet, all the soldiers were rounded up like so many military Willie Winkies, to be in bed for 10 o'clock. It was our first taste of army 'rules and regs', but not our last.

Some while later, I worked my last Saturday at Woolworth's in George Street. With my new job it was now much more difficult to fit everything in, as I had to make my way home from the harbour at lunch time, then be at the shop for 1.30. In a way, I was sorry to leave, but I was earning a better wage by this time, and I would have Saturday afternoons free to follow my own pursuits. My chum Peggy Walker stayed on, and we would meet up as usual for our Sunday outings, walks, nights at the pictures, and other events in the social calendar. Woolies was busy as usual that Saturday, with many servicemen among the crowds. I heard a voice enquire, 'What are you doing tonight?'. Looking up, I was surprised to see a soldier in battledress, with cap showing the badge of the Gordon Highlanders. It was the same lad that had so annoyed me at the dance hall. I made a barbed remark and continued attending to the customers, but he was so persistent that finally, when the shop closed, I walked out into the pitch dark with my khaki-clad escort and boarded a tram (its lights dimmed by dark blue globes), for an evening at the Astoria. There we watched one of the 'Blondie and Dagmar' films – American, of course – and sang the latest songs to the accompaniment of the organ, which my companion seemed to enjoy very much, no doubt being quite unused to such entertainment. We returned to my house door by tram, and my mother called out, 'Bring the sodger in for a cup of tea'. Normally this would not have happened with someone I had just met, but the war was already changing our attitudes. Seeming not to notice my considerable discomfiture, my companion eagerly accepted the invitation. 'A nice loon', my mother commented when he departed, having assured her that he had coppers for the tram, and having been given directions to find his billet at Skene Square School in the blackout. And that was that, or so I thought.

America labelled this period the 'Phoney War'. There seemed as yet to be nothing happening in France, and the skies over Britain were clear of bombers from Germany, but this country waited as Poland was battered and besieged by the Nazi hordes, the Poles fighting magnificently but unavailingly to save their country. At sea, also, the battle against enemy U-boats was in full swing, with severe loss of tonnage among our merchant fleet as it struggled to bring food to our shores. At home, gas masks were issued to everybody, with the instruction that they be carried at all times. Those for adults were of plain design, supplied in small cardboard boxes, while children's ones, due to their colour, made the wearer look like Mickey Mouse, much to the general amusement and to the abatement of fear. In fact we all ended up laughing at the bizarre picture that we made. For very young infants there was a fearsome-looking contraption in which they could lie. Leatherette cases with zip top and handle were available in the shops to facilitate the carrying of masks, so it was 'handbag and gas mask' wherever we went. Chemical warfare had begun in the trenches during the first World War, and no-one knew whether Hitler might launch such an attack against British cities. Warning of a gas raid was to be given by ARP wardens with rattles giving out a loud sound not unlike a corn-crake. Practice-runs were common, and we quickly got used to those and to the sinister wail of the air-raid siren.

The 'Phoney War' period was a great time for complaining. People complained about almost anything, but most of all the blackout, in which accidents became much more frequent as the dark nights of winter drew on. Lampposts, pillar boxes, telephone boxes, uneven pavements and high kerbs were the hidden enemy as people walked about almost blindly, despite the universal carrying of hand torches. Black eyes and injured noses always raised a laugh, cruel though it may sound, and inquiries as to how the mishap occurred were often answered with 'I wisna even drunk at the time'!.

At work, we girls gained a new interest – anti-aircraft ('ack-ack') gun emplacements had been installed along the quays, and were manned by groups of soldiers who whistled and called at us as we went by. The guns pointed to the sky in readiness, and the time would come when we would hear them in action. Steel helmeted soldiers lounged around smoking, glad of some relief from the boredom through exchange of repartee with the girls who worked in the area. It was our habit to have mid-morning and mid-afternoon tea-breaks, although because we were on piece-work these were kept short. One day, someone had the brilliant idea of inviting two or three of the soldiers up to our work-place for a cup of tea and a biscuit. This rather dismayed Jimmy, our gaffer, but we pointed out, 'It's for the war effort, Jimmy', and that gentle man smiled in agreement, although in permitting us to have some entertaining male company he did not allow the work of trawl net-making to suffer.

Girl talk, as busy hands flew at the nets, usually centred on love and romance. The word 'sex' was not used as it is now, neither was it seen in print in newspapers or the women's magazines of the time. Even in certain Sunday newspapers, it was the term 'intimate relationship' that told all when some story broke regarding a breach of promise case or the like, usually concerning some member of the upper classes. At this time in the war, in fact, love and romance bloomed. Tears were shed by workmates whose husbands were sent off to France, marriages became more frequent (as was evidenced by the picture pages of the local weekly paper 'Bon-Accord'), and banns were called at short notice for members of the armed forces. Gracie Fields, the Lancashire lass, sang 'Wish Me Luck As You Wave Me Goodbye', and Vera Lynn, soon to be named 'the forces' sweetheart', whose clear, rather plaintive voice we would come to know so well, was heard on the wireless epitomising in her songs the thoughts of many a couple parted by the war.

Not that all was sadness. The wittier, more cynical characters in our midst were always on hand to cause laughter. A wedding-page photograph of a bride who looked like an Amazon alongside her rather diminutive husband brought a ribald comment or two – 'She'll hae t' peen 'im t' the pillow!', and 'He'll go up wi' the blind in the mornin'!'. Might there perhaps have been a little trace of envy in some of these remarks, coming from girls – indeed women – as yet unmarried? I rather suspect so, as for most females in those days marriage was the only goal in life, and we younger ones (I was still only 17) dreamed of some tall, dark, handsome chap who would come along and sweep us off our feet. He would of course now be in the armed forces, be that the Army, the Navy (which I rather fancied) or the Air Force, who, in their nice blue uniforms, had been christened 'the Brylcreem boys'. 'How do we know when we fall in love? How do we know when it's the real thing?' These were questions often asked of our more worldly-wise associates, who in reply would quote some magazine informing the anxious female that love was 'a chemistry that would be recognised at once'. Sometimes when Jimmy came up the wooden steps from the riggers' yard he must have wondered what we were all laughing at. When he was present, the girls pleased him by singing – they were happy times, and he loved the 'choruses', as the girls called them. In his absence, however, risqué jokes and ribald comments flew around until his return, when all went quiet again, although laughter was never far away.

That November there came an opportunity to attend another ATS dance, this time at the Music Hall. My workmate Mary McHattie had managed to obtain six tickets, and no black-out was going to deter us from going – in fact, the war-time atmosphere made it all even more exciting. 'What on earth will I wear?' This cry was by now very familiar to my mother, who, as with mothers everywhere, had plenty of other things to think about – ration books, points for biscuits, the poor quality of children's shoes, etc. – but she did muster enough enthusiasm to suggest a blue dress that she had shortened for me to make it more fashionable. I had a nice new winter coat in what was called 'petrel blue', with fur-trimmed collar, and I would proudly wear this when 'utility garments', all so very much the same, came to be all that was available in the shops.

That night, we entered the Music Hall's blackout curtained doorway, surveyed our prospects, then made for the cloakroom to apply some vanishing cream, a little dab of powder, and some 'kiss-proof' lipstick (as worn by the stars, of course). Once ready, we joined the throng, males on one side and females on the other, as usual. A sea of khaki met the eye, and in the midst of it I spotted Bill, the soldier who I had met at the Abergeldie and who had taken me to the Astoria a little while before. My chums Mary and Peggy gave me a nudge of encouragement – 'Here's your soldier chappie again!' He was not exactly tall, dark and handsome, but he was taller than me, blue eyed and fair haired, quite good looking in his uniform, and a very good dancer.

As it happened, I had various partners during the evening, but no last dance from my 'soldier chappie', as, he explained, he had a girl with him and would have to see her home. 'Fit a cheek, telling me that', I exclaimed to the girls. He was right back at the bottom of the scale in my estimation, and no mistake. 'At least he was honest', they replied, which was true, but love at first sight this wasn't. At work the next day we spoke about the dance, and about further similar evenings that we had lined up. We were determined that our social life would go on, even though the sky every night was lit up by criss-crossing searchlight beams, and barrage balloons floated like great bulbous airships as the drill of being prepared went on unceasingly.

My uncle Georgie had two workmates, Frank Mitchell and Bill Cooper, who sometimes came to our house. They once accompanied myself and my chums, Betty and Peggy, to a party, and we often met up 'on the mat'. With these two nice lads, we went first-footing at Hogmanay 1939, to Aunt Daisy's as usual before walking all the way to Seaton where one of the lads lived. The next night we all went to the Majestic in Union Street to see what turned out to be rather a dreary film about Flanders – not the happiest of efforts, although there was a second feature to cheer us up. Soon after, Bill was in the Navy, at a training barracks in the south of England, and Frank was in the Army. Enthusiastic letters full of Navy jargon arrived from our new recruit, who, like almost all young lads who had never been away before, was hungry for home news. I soon became conversant with expressions like 'Chief ERA' (Engine Room Artificer), the 'heads' (toilets) and 'gash' (rubbish).

On the mat one Sunday, Peggy and I met up with some lads home on their first leave from square-bashing in the Army. We were standing talking when a voice boomed out – 'Get that collar buttoned up, you slovenly shower!' And that wasn't all. That Sergeant-Major may have been short of stature, but he wasn't short of words as he gave those lads a roasting which left no-one in any doubt as to what was what in the Army. 'Black affrontit', we said afterwards, but it was a glimpse of the kind of discipline that made our fighting forces the best in the world.

Top: The net braiders, Albert Quay, 1940. I am on the far left, at the back.
In the right foreground is Jimmy, the foreman
Centre: With friend Peggy Walker, c. 1940 – note the headgear!
Bottom: The munition workers' training class, 1942
(I am in the front row, far right)

CHAPTER 4

In February 1940, our family moved house yet again. Chief instigator in this was my brother James, who had never liked his new school, and still very much missed his friends in Fittie and the closeness of the sea. I didn't miss any of that; I was more than happy to have space and a bathroom, etc., instead of the former cramped conditions, and I had lots of other things to occupy me. However, an opportunity presented itself in the form of an exchange advertised in the Aberdeen Evening Express, and one cold and snowy afternoon James and my mother went to view the house that was on offer. After two tram-rides and a brisk walk, they arrived at Kaimhill, where the red-tiled sloping roofs of the recently-built houses gave the area an attractive appearance even on that wintry day. An agreement was reached, the exchange was made, and the move began. On the first day I arrived from work, grumbling about the new route home which entailed a long tram ride to the Bridge of Dee and a cold walk from beside the dog-racing track. I found the family, assisted by Georgie and some of Andrew's friends, laying the lino after having worked frantically to cover the windows before blackout-time, the hour of which was printed daily in the newspapers. Along with the others, I took an immediate liking to the house, which we felt had a friendly atmosphere. Situated at the end of a terraced villa-type row of four houses, it had front and side doors and a fair-sized garden, while its front overlooked a bank of well laid-out bushes and young trees. The living room was at the rear, there was a front room with a large window, and the lower floor was completed with a small kitchen. The longish hallway connected the front door with the kitchen and living room. Upstairs were two bedrooms and the bathroom. It was a very nice modern house in an area where at one time, when I was a small girl, my mother had taken us on the subbie train for picnics.

There were other changes to come during 1940. Winston Churchill became Prime Minister, and the 'phoney war' ended. The Germans began to bomb military targets, resulting in civilian casualties (40 were killed in London in the first air attacks, it was reported), and the stepping up of the evacuation of children from London and other major cities. During the 'phoney war', many women and children, evacuated at the war's outset, returned to their homes, but when the air raids began they had to go back to the country. The Home Guard (formerly the Land Defence Volunteers, or LDV), made up of older men, was to be seen parading and practising, its members obviously relishing their role of home front protectors, and happy to be 'doing their bit' for the war effort.

Many foods were becoming increasingly scarce, but fish was still readily available. Grannie brought us some flounders caught in the bay from Granda's boatie, and very welcome they were. The local name for them was 'flatties' or 'flukies'. Granny very much liked our new abode. It was 'affa' fine', and she trekked over there frequently each week, walking to the city centre and boarding the No 1 tram to the bridge. The walk from there to Kaimhill was 'nae bother at a'; it kept her fit, she said. An energetic, hard-working lady was our Grandma Masson, who, unless she was knitting, never sat around if there were other things to do. She had a sharp tongue for things of which she disapproved ('skirts too short, heels too high!'), but her criticisms carried little weight. She was in fact quite fashionable in her own choice of apparel, though most of her 'best' was kept for church on Sundays. Since moving to her single room in Fittie with Granda and their dog, Bruce, she had had her long brown hair shorn into a bob style which she said was much easier to work with nowadays. Granda, meanwhile, had succeeded in finding a job at Hall Russell's shipyard, not, I believe, in his trade of ship's carpenter, but as an odd-jobber around the yards. He was neverthless happy to be out of retirement and fully occupied once again. Daisy over in Torry also had visits from Granny, who liked to be kept in the picture regarding the doings of the family. Georgie, stationed at Arbroath with his Army unit, was quite lucky in being so near to home.

At this time there began a new craze which was to more than rival that for card games in the home. Every house now had a dart-board, except of course for those in which extra value was put on the appearance of walls and doors. Those darts played havoc at first, but such was the game's popularity that it soon came to be accommodated by the making of special shields and frames, thus saving much pitted woodwork and chipped plaster. It may perhaps be a little difficult to visualise life without television, but social life and family get-togethers at home with games of cards or darts, or just conversation over a cup of tea, could be very enjoyable.

Outings to the Tivoli and HM Theatres or to the pictures were still very much on the agenda, even though proceedings might be interrupted by the appearance on screen (in the cinemas, at least) of a special slide announcing 'Air Raid Warning' and intimating that patrons wishing to leave the theatre or cinema were free to do so. Not many ever did leave – as we young folk said, 'We've paid our money; we'll see the programme'! It was well known that these buildings were well reinforced, and that firewatchers trained in dealing with incendiaries were on station. There were many hit-and-run raids on the city, and although these were by lone bombers coming in over the North Sea, they still resulted in casualties. When Holland, Belgium and then Norway succumbed to the Nazis, bombings became more frequent, especially from Norway, which provided a very convenient base for the Luftwaffe to mount much heavier raids on the city, and at that point things became far worse.

'Creelings' occurred quite often now at my place of work as brides-to-be had nets thrown over their heads and were rolled over and over on the floor until everyone was exhausted with laughter, the bride eventually disentangling herself from the mesh. No leave of absence was given for weddings; one simply got married then came straight back to work. The bridegroom, meanwhile, would report back to his unit after a brief honeymoon during which the couple's time together was confined to outwith working hours. There was of course the usual week's local holiday in July, but the armed forces did not take account of such things in the handing out of leave slips. 'There's a war on!' – as if anyone needed reminding.

Public places were full of posters, most of them warning of the need to guard against careless conversation in case something was overheard by a spy, and certainly 'Lord Haw-Haw' always seemed to know what was going on in Britain when his immaculate English tones were beamed to our radios by the powerful propaganda transmitters of the Third Reich. His real name was William Joyce, and he was the worst of all traitors, endeavouring to break morale through psychological warfare against his own country. He always seemed to know which ships had been sunk and just where others were anchored as, against a background of food shortages in Britain, he tried to stoke the doubts and fears of people at home, and to make the German blockade appear more and more successful.

As 1940 went on, virtually all commodities came to be rationed and queuing for food became a way of life. A large family such as ours had a corresponding number of ration books, so that although individual quantities were small, those ounces of tea, sugar, bacon, butter or margarine gave us considerable scope for meals. As I have already mentioned, many of the recipients of ration books were people who during the Depression of the 1930s had never had enough to eat. Now, with more work available and consequently a little more money, they were able to afford those small weekly rations. Furthermore, anyone who had coupons to spare (principally the clothes coupons which came later in the war) could sell them. Thus the 'black market' came about, together with the 'spiv' that operated it.

'Here's a bittie butter', my mother would say to Granny, who would then go home with an ounce or two of the precious commodity, or perhaps with some sugar, but that was often very scarce in our house, as we liked to have it in our tea. On occasion we even ran to a 'clootie dumpling'. 'Ahhh...!' - we were like the Bisto Kids as we came in through the door and were met by that delicious smell from the kitchen. Mother's clooties were the best ever – sweet and filling, large and sliceable. What a treat they were.

We danced the Lambeth Walk, which was a new innovation from a London show. Every dance hall was crowded at night with young people, and every kind of uniform was to be seen in the throng. Live bands beat out the music, and the air raid siren didn't bother us.

So in these extraordinary times the family settled into its new abode. One bedroom was minus its linoleum, and all we could do was to stain and varnish the floorboards. No carpets or rugs could be bought; similarly, wallpaper was an impossibility. The word 'stipple' came into our vocabulary when we turned our attention to decorating the walls. First a coat of distemper was applied, then, while it was still wet, a pattern of sorts was added by dabbing another colour on top with a rag, an old sponge, or simply a rolled-up newspaper. This task was without doubt the most unpopular of all, but, pleased with what she described as 'fresh and a nice change', mother would proceed to one room after the other and the stippling would begin all over again. With luck and a little practice, the results could indeed be remarkably good. The two colours gave a nice bright effect, and we decorated the whole house apart from the kitchen in this supposedly makeshift way which, I notice, still makes its appearance in what we now call 'interior design'! Windows were made more troublesome than ever to paint by the demands of the blackout. Careful work and timing were required, otherwise the ARP warden's whistle would sound, or we might hear his knock at the door, which made us all feel thoroughly guilty.

Our door was never locked. The latch key was kept on a string so that it could be pulled through the letter box when required, but that was seldom. We found our new neighbours to be the salt of the earth, friendly and helpful in every way. Next door was the Reid family, consisting of a widowed mother and three daughters (she did in fact have a fourth daughter, who was married, with two children). Stout and of a jolly disposition, Mrs Reid never left the house. The three girls seemed to have a good but casual relationship with their mother, who appeared not to mind at all their rather untidy habits. Gladys, who, I think, worked in an office, was a very striking-looking real platinum blonde with a good figure. Cathie was of stout build and resembled her mother in her cheery demeanour; she seemed rather a studious type, with a liking for classical music. Winnie, the youngest, was a nice looking girl, smaller of build than the others. Judging by the number of times that we heard 'Begin the Beguine' and 'Deep Purple' on their gramophone, they really loved these numbers!

Next door to the Reids were the Wilsons, whose two married daughters lived with them. I seem to recollect that they also had three sons, the youngest of whom was still at school. Mrs Wilson, a comely quick-talking woman, kept a busy house much the same as ours. Her husband Dave was the subject of much sympathy although nothing was ever said in his presence. He had come home from the Great War shell-shocked and trembling, and had never recovered. A poor man who would never work again, he had nonetheless great spirit and would attend to chores around the house with his devoted wife and family. He had no pension, and the family lived frugally on solely what the state allowed them. They were a nice family. Their eldest daughter was named Nettie, and her husband was somewhere in North Africa with the Army. They had no children, but her sister Chrissie, whose husband was an AC2 in the Air Force, had two, so it was a large household.

Mrs Wilson had, like most housewives, to base her menu on the usual dried egg and Spam (which, incidentally, was brought in from America), but sometimes she would be inspired and would rush in with a dish of fish pie or bread pudding. 'Isn't this a rare breid pudding!' she would say; it was usually made with dried milk, a few pieces of dried fruit and some stale bread, but like so many of these 'concoctions' it was remarkably good to eat.

At the opposite end of our block, which had sloping gardens and a handy concrete path giving each family easy access to one another, lived the Ross family. Mrs Ross hailed from Edinburgh. Stout of build and somewhat lofty in her mode of speech, she was a cheery soul. She had two daughters, the elder (Margaret) soon to be married, and a younger married daughter with two children. She also had a young son. We got to know other families nearby – there were the Stewarts next to our back garden, and the Annands, a large family, mostly grown up but with some small grandchildren. Of course, in the usual way of Aberdonians they would be known as 'Stewartie' and 'Rossie'. Good people all of them.

One evening, the Ross family held a party at which all the teenagers and young married folk got together. Gladys, our blonde from the Reid family, brought along her current boyfriend, an Army officer. Not in the slightest overawed by him, we played all the usual party games, including pinning the tail on the donkey, plus, the company being mixed, several kissing games. There were the usual soft drinks, and Mrs Ross provided some of her home baking which she always seemed to be able to make despite rationing.

Rationing was in fact to become much more rigorous before long. At this time such things as clothing were still quite readily available, but the time was coming when the lives of our merchant seamen would no longer be risked to import such non-essentials, and the ration books would have to come out. A look at the George Street fashion shops showed us the new styles for 1940. I seem to remember predominantly dark materials being in evidence, with perhaps a small printed floral pattern for dresses. These had 'leg of mutton'-style short sleeves and I didn't care for them at all, but

48

choice was limited, and that was life in the war.

Fine weather in early spring brought with it thoughts of a picnic for our net-braiders. A Sunday outing to Persley Den was arranged, and a crowd of us, armed with sandwiches, etc, made its way to what was then quite a quiet beauty spot beside the River Don. We were all quite glad to sit down after clambering through the thick bushes that separated the Den from the roadway where we had alighted from the tramcar. We ate lunch and had just enjoyed a wade in the dark waters of the river when the Spring sunshine suddenly disappeared and we received a reminder of the vagaries of the Scottish climate – a monsoon-like deluge which was made worse by the fact that we had all come away without any protection against the elements. Soaking and bedraggled, we made our way back up the now-slippery slopes of the woods, to the shelter of the tram and home again, myself to a blissful hot bath. We had no weather warnings like there are now, and there was quite some sneezing and sniffling on the Monday morning!

At work, I took to walking with the Fittie girls when they went home for dinner break. Since I moved house, Grandma Masson had offered me a plate of soup or some such sustenance at lunchtimes, so back I would go each day along the old familiar streets. With the girls, I walked through the Fish Market, over the lock gate bridge at Wellington Street and into Fittie. Wolf whistles from the many Navy ships in the harbour would echo around us as we walked along, and we would often see, to our amusement, sailors being drilled or exercised on the Fish Market's concrete floor. Most of them were members of minesweeper crews. Working in very cramped conditions aboard ship, they looked rather a motley lot, dressed in working gear and often clumping around in short sea-boots, although they always wore their caps. As we passed, the drill tended to be interrupted, but then the men were not square-bashing, only stretching their legs. We did not mind at all; it was all part of the war-time adventure.

I still wrote letters to, and received letters from, the Naval Store Barracks. I was trying to cheer up these homesick lads who just a short while ago had been walking the mat or dancing with us at one or another of the city's ballrooms, and in return I received newsy, friendly letters in which I enjoyed reading of my friends' new environment. Bill Cooper sent me a nice gold watch plus indications of a desire that we should have a more serious association later on. While not unappreciative of the gift, I offered to return it as I had at that time no intention of being tied down to anyone in particular, but we still exchanged a few letters before our sailor boy went off on his first ship. Frank Mitchell, who was in the Army, I was never to see again.

In George Street, near to Reid and Pearson's, there appeared a new shop which was constantly crowded. This was Jerome's, one of many photographers' studios of that name, set up to cater for a brisk war-time market. Cheaply turned-out photos of soldiers, sailors and airmen were taken for sending to loved ones away from home or in other cities – mementos to be framed, cherished and admired by relatives. 'Oh, isn't he smart in his uniform!' I still have a few such photos from this shop.

Most of our ration books were registered at the Mannofield Co-op, quite a walk away, although walks never bothered my mother. Registration was demanded by the new coalition Goverment under Winston Churchill. Rations were generally bought once a week, which posed no problem for dry goods, but such things as butter, margarine and meat were not so easy to keep. Nowadays refrigerators take care of that, but such appliances were not exactly common in 1940. Truth to say, we could have eaten our entire week's meat ration in one day, but there were other foods with which we could meet our culinary needs – the good old dried egg powder, fish, vegetable pie, and sausages, which were known as 'breadcrumbs in battledress'. No doubt it was also during this period that they also became popularly referred to as 'mystery bags'!

Whenever my mother spoke of shifting furniture in our new house (and she often did), arguments would develop, usually ending in my sister and I pushing and shoving things around, trying to keep our patience with my mother's insatiable urge to make the place look different. We didn't really mind until we came to our old box-topped sewing machine, which actually belonged to Granny, and on which my mother had made our dresses and trouses when we were children. She still used it, so up the stairs it had to go to one of the bedrooms, a task of Herculean proportions, accompanied by much puffing, panting and fraying of tempers. Too cold in the bedroom. Down we trachled with it again. Come the warmer weather, a blank refusal to go through the whole process again was not kindly received by Mother, who, in her determination, tried to haul the machine upstairs herself, and would have done so if my brother had not come to her aid. 'Nae bother wi' my loons', she told Mrs Wilson, 'But that two quinies are aye arguin''.

Near our house in Kaimhill was a small hut shop which sold lovely white floury baps, bread, milk and certain things off ration. Another shop opened nearby in competition; it was not as convenient as the small shop but was more of a grocer's, and periodically we and other regular customers would register surplus ration books with its proprietor, Mr Greig, known of course as 'Griggie'. He returned the favour by reserving for us the occasional 'under-the counter' item. Beginning with cigarettes, beer, whisky and sweets, some commodities had now all but disappeared, and others were in such short supply that the arrangement was well worthwhile. 'We'll try Griggie's' was a phrase often heard among the folk of Kaimhill in those days of shortage, but it was all perfectly above board, and had nothing to do with the black market.

I paid my second visit to HM Theatre in company with Cathie Reid from next door, who had so wanted to see and hear the great Richard Tauber. It was exciting to sit there in the stalls and to hear Tauber sing 'You Are My Heart's Delight', followed by encore after encore. He received a standing ovation from the audience, which included many service people; it was my only outing with Cathie, but I have never forgotten the enjoyment we had. At the Tivoli Theatre in Guild Street, the scenario was different. Variety programmes played to packed houses, with the Glaswegian comic Dave Willis a great favourite. His ARP warden act was hilarious. Dressed in that uniform complete with steel helmet and gas mask, and singing about 'An airyplane, an airyplane, away-way up-a-ky', which was so topical, he fairly brought the house down. My father always went to see him when he could.

At about this time, my father took to looking in at the Bridge Of Dee Bar for a couple of beers on his way home, a thing that he would never have done previously and never did after the war. The family did not like it very much, but it was realised that if his job at sea had been dangerous before, it was even more so now that trawlers were sitting targets for German hit-and-run bombers, which could appear with frightening suddenness. We saw poignant evidence of this one day while at work on Albert Quay. Word went round during our forenoon tea-break that a badly crippled trawler was making its way into port, and down we ran to watch it struggle into its berth. In silence, we stood as the ship came in with most of its bridge and superstructure gone and wreckage strewn about its deck. It had been a large trawler, probably from Grimsby, but it didn't seem like a ship any more, and few of its crew had survived what had obviously been a bomb attack. It was my first sight of such tragedy, and we all felt shaken and sad as we trooped back to work.

During the early part of 1940, my friend Peggy Walker and I went out on occasional dates with one member or another of HM Forces. Neither of us had thoughts of any serious attachment; we preferred freedom to enjoy our teenage lifestyle in this city that had so much to offer. Then, early one evening outside the Grand Central Cinema (the 'Grandie') in George Street, we were debating whether to go in and see the film, and were just about to do so when two soldiers came up and spoke to us. One I recognised as Bill, whom I had last seen at the Music Hall dance. In the course of the conversation, he told me that he was going home on leave, and that he would be 21 years of age that April. He asked me where I now lived, as he had called at my old address, and I answered in a rather detached manner, anxious to get in for the start of the picture. Peggy, meanwhile, spoke in similar fashion with the other chap. 'So long, see you later', we said, and with that we left them.

Some days later, on a Saturday afternoon, I answered a knock on our front door, and there stood Bill, carrying a small parcel. 'I brought this for your mother', he said. Invited in, he handed it to her. It contained a chicken which he had brought from his home, a smallholding where they kept a lot of poultry. 'Come back and bring a pal', my mother said when he left. This was now common practice among the good folk of our district, who filled their homes with lonely young soldiers and other members of the armed forces, sharing with them the comfort of home, rations and company. In that way, many 'got their feet under the table' (as the saying went), until wartime requirements moved them on to camp, barracks, another town, or perhaps to France, where the British European Forces were languishing near the Maginot Line. On his next visit, Bill brought with him a fellow soldier with whom he had struck up a strong friendship. More of a townie, being from Cambuslang near Glasgow, 'Big Wull' (Willie Young) had been a butcher, working in the Co-op, and was now an Army cook. A big, dark-haired lad, he had an earnest expression which belied a typically Glaswegian sense of humour. His father was a coalminer, and he had an elder sister, but he was the only son in the family, and he amused us by speaking of his 'Mammy and Daddy' at home.

This friendship between Bill and Wull would last for many, many years. War had this effect on people, drawing together neighbours, families and friends in a bond that presented a united face against the unprecedented dangers that had come into all our lives. Many 'goodies' came via Wull from his very generous mother. Home-made dumpling in a large tin, sweets (now very scarce indeed) and cakes arrived regularly on our table, and letters came from Mr and Mrs Young expressing sincere gratitude for giving a home-from-home to their son, who they so much missed and worried over. However, it was Bill Kilgour who, through sheer determination and perseverance, made it known that I was the girl for him. Romance blossomed enough for me to begin asking myself, as I remembered from the girls' magazine at work, 'Was this love, this chemistry between us?'. But there was not yet any question of abandoning my regular social pursuits. Peggy and I still teamed up as before, but I set apart evenings for picture-going and other dates with Bill, although servicemen, when not required to perform such things as guard duty, had to apply for passes out, and there was no guarantee that these would be granted.

Well paid the boys weren't, but they were still expected to set aside 7s 6d each week for their next of kin, and that left very little money to rattle in their pockets. Both Wull and Bill smoked cigarettes, which I believe were available quite cheaply in the NAAFI canteen. When my father's ship went out beyond the three mile limit, he and the rest of the crew were given a bonded cigarette allowance, and he used to give a few to the lads when he could. A generous man when he had a few extra shillings, he would often stand Bill his tram fares; after all, he said, he had been a soldier too! Quite how my mother managed to feed everyone who came to our house I don't know, but she did. There were those that had rations to spare and would not share with others, but neither we nor our neighbours were like that – I remember especially the Annand family, whose house near to ours was always full to the gunwales. Bill and Wullie were the first of many servicemen who were invited into our home at Kaimhill, to sit at our table with the family, usually on the strength of 'I am a cousin/friend/brother-in-law, etc, and this is my pal'. So it went on through the dark days of the war.

At the end of May 1940 came the debacle of Dunkirk, leading to the dramatic rescue of thousands of British and Allied troops from the beaches as the Germans swept through France, trying to encircle the retreating armies. France's capitulation and the declaration of Paris as an open city came as a cruel blow, causing the armies to have to fight their way out. At home, the news of the disaster was received with the usual calm resignation, but also with a great deal of anger towards the French, especially when the newspapers began to print long lists of casualties and those taken prisoner-of-war.

The story is well known of how 'the little boats' were pressed into service to take all these men to safety while German planes strafed and bombarded them. At St Valery, there was a mass taking of prisoners by the Germans, mostly Scots of the 51st Highland Division, who fought all the way but were unable to escape to the coast. At work, I well remember the stoic demeanour of the young women who came in to work at their nets while grieving for relatives taken prisoner or worse. A word or two of sympathy, then they were respectfully left to their own thoughts.

In the aftermath of Dunkirk, many new types of servicemen were to be seen on our busy streets. Unfamiliar shoulder flashes proclaimed them as Free French, Free Dutch, Polish, Czech, etc, who had come to these shores when their countries were overrun. Uniforms were everywhere, even down to the telegram boys who raced around on red bikes, delivering messages in yellow envelopes. The railway station in Guild Street was always full of people boarding trains or alighting, to be met by their loved ones who had probably waited for hours as train after train, all laden, steamed in. 'Is Your Journey Really Necessary?' demanded the posters at the station. 'Go To It'; 'Loose Lips Sink Ships'; 'Careless Talk Costs Lives'; we needed no reminding of the war – the evidence was all around us.

Soon these new uniformed men were seen at the pictures and in the dance halls, many enjoying the hospitality shown to them in North-East homes. They also shared the danger from the North Sea when the German hit-and-run raiders came. The Polish soldiers in particular had impeccable manners which thrilled the young girls. In the ballroom, with a click of the heels and a little bow they would ask, 'You dance with me, yes?' The conversation usually stopped there, and at the end of the number the partner was seen back to her seat with another click of the heels, a bow, and a 'thank you'. Naturally, this made a great topic of conversation at work the next day. Such a pity that we could never hope to understand the language of these gallant lads!

When, in June 1940, Italy entered the war and we stood alone against what was now the Axis of Fascist powers, Mussolini was universally ridiculed, even in children's comics ('Musso the Wop, he's a big-a-da flop'). Similarly, Adolph, portrayed as a weak little figure, stood no chance against Pansy Potter, the Strongman's Daughter. As soon as Italy made its move, Winston Churchill gave the order 'Collar the lot!', and Italians living in Britain who had for any reason failed to take out nationalisation papers were immediately interned. Our friendly, hard-working ice cream men, café owners, etc, so well-known to us through the years, suddenly disappeared 'for the duration', many to the Isle Of Man where they languished, classed as enemies of our country.

Security around the harbour area was stepped up, and in addition to pass cards we had at all times to carry our identity cards, which bore our names and numbers – my number was SUA1 37/3. The dire threat of invasion was a central topic of conversation and speculation as we waited for Hitler to turn from his triumphs in Europe to vent his wrath on this island. Every morning at work we wondered 'Will the invasion begin to-day?', but life still went on. One night at our house, Wullie donned his steel helmet and played war-games with my small brothers and sisters. They hid behind the settee and pounced on Wullie but never beat him – he was the British soldier and they were the Germans! The kids thought it all great fun.

On the wireless, we listened to Churchill's speeches; 'We will fight them on the streets, we will fight them on the beaches... we will never surrender' – what stirring times these were. Newsreaders such as Alvar Liddell, Stuart Hibberd and Bruce Belfrage were now household names. Among the messages which their solemn tones conveyed to an avidly listening nation was the silencing of all church bells except as warning of the much-feared invasion which the Germans were known to be planning. Not that it was all doom and gloom. Laughter came over the airwaves as well, most notably in the tremendously popular show ITMA ('It's That Man Again'), in which the much-loved Tommy Handley portrayed such characters as Funf the German spy and Mrs Mopp ('Can I do you now, sir?').

On the day-to-day domestic front, new recipes went the rounds of ourselves and our neighbours. Such dishes as the meatless Woolton pie (called after Lord Woolton, the Minister of Food) were typical, while excellent eggless cakes were baked by the expert Mrs Ross for afternoon fly-cups, and Mrs Wilson excelled at syrup puddings and potato puddings.

Money was one of the scarcest commodities, while such essentials as shoes deteriorated alarmingly in quality and had to be replaced all the more often. Worst were children's shoes, which seemed only to last for a few weeks; I remember my mother exclaiming, 'I think they're made of cardboard!' as she despairingly reviewed the footwear situation. Of course we knew that the armed forces had to have priority, but we also knew that somewhere there were factory owners making a fortune from the manufacture of army boots and uniforms. My grandmother considered army greatcoats to be 'A' weight an' nae warmth', and I suspect that she was right. Regular British Army uniforms were made of strong, rough material and were classed as 'battledress'. Officers' dress uniforms were tailored at their own expense, and had smart trousers, jacket of finer khaki material, and caps of the elegant visor ('cheesecutter') type, except in the Highland regiments, which had caps of a different design. Winston Churchill himself introduced the 'siren suit', a simple garment which could be easily slipped on in a hurry in the event of an air raid. Churchill was to wear his often during the blitz-filled times to come.

With the first winter of the war well behind us, relief was to be clearly seen on the faces of people travelling to work each morning. In the bright July sun, the tram 'carries' seemed so much cheerier as they trundled into town, their faint blue interior lamps no longer needed. Everything had been so dark and dreary, but now there was still daylight even at the end of work, making pocket-torches a necessity only when coming home from the pictures or from the dancing much later. With only this small beam of light to relieve the darkness and to help avoid black eyes and skinned noses, we girls walked home or caught the tram on even the darkest night. Servicemen abounded in the city, but we were never troubled by any of them. The penalties for crime in the forces were to say the least severe, and we never had any worries. Indeed, we would often walk along with soldiers who had missed their bus, bidding them goodnight and hoping that they would make it back to camp before reveille!

Evidence of the seriousness of Hitler's invasion threat seemed to spring out at us wherever we went. The beach was now covered in large concrete blocks and barbed wire defences, part of a protective 'fence' that extended all the way around the coastline of Britain. Strewn about the sands in an apparently haphazard fashion, the blocks looked ugly and untidy, but we all knew why they were there.

Air raid shelters were everywhere. Many were of the large concrete variety, while some houses had small Anderson shelters dug into their gardens. In our area there was no room for either, so for the present time the cupboard under our stairs, small as it was, had to do. To this end it was equipped with a battery lamp - a little frosted glass affair in the shape of an owl, whose eyes stared unblinkingly at the scene as we huddled fearfully in the small space. If all the family was at home, the children would be given priority in this the only shelter we had, while the rest of us had simply to trust in providence.

The fall of Norway gave Germany an excellent opportunity to make Scotland's ports a prime and easy target. One bright July morning in 1940 I walked down Market Street and on to the quays as usual, meeting up with some of my workmates on the way. We waved good morning to the sailors whose ships (mainly minesweepers) were closely berthed in the Albert Basin. Some of these small minesweepers had been out during the night making safe the Channel so that the Merchant Fleet could join up in convoys. The ack-ack crews at the harbour also received a cheery word and a wave from us, and we went about our work very happily that morning. Why all this cheer? It was the 12th of July, the beginning of Trades Week – a whole week's holiday (albeit unpaid), during which we could have a nice lazy time at home, go to the pictures or go dancing, which was just about all that most of us could afford. Each of us hurried to finish her own piece of net, which, with the assistance of the others, she rolled and folded for the riggers downstairs to incorporate in the completed product. A celebratory tea was organised, with biscuits purchased with some ration points from a small shop nearby.

All had just been made ready when one of the riggers warned us of an early alert. This was very closely followed by the ominous wail of the sirens, and in the silence after that we could hear the drone of a plane. 'Sounds like one of theirs', someone said. All of a sudden, what sounded like every gun on the ships and on the quayside opened fire, surrounding us with a terrifying, ear-splitting cacophony of noise. There was panic as instinct propelled us all towards the door and the wooden stairs to the ground level. Women and girls, white-faced and shaking, joined the men underneath the loft-like building – and then the bombs fell.

I swear that we could actually hear those implements of death and destruction rattle from the bomb racks of the planes. Next came the screaming whistle and the terrific ground-shaking explosion as each bomb found its target. Shrapnel from the guns rained down on the roof of our make-shift shelter as we stood huddled together, not hysterical but silent as each explosion blasted the air. Nine bombs, we later heard, fell on Hall Russell's shipyard as the men were having their dinner break. Only the small expanse of water in the harbour divided us from this terrible scene, and we could hardly believe that we had escaped unscathed.

Forty men died in the shipyard that day, and the German bomber, chased and shot at by Spitfires, was brought down near Kaimhill, crashing into the unfinished skating rink building on Anderson Drive. I heard the full story when I arrived home, full of anxiety after having been told that the plane had been brought down so close to our house. My mother and sister had watched from the stair-top window as the Heinkel was chased across the city. 'It came in so low', my mother said, 'that we could see the big black crosses on the wings, and the guns were firing. It seemed to come towards our house, so we ran downstairs. Then we heard the crash.'

My grandmother had been alone in her house in Fittie when the raid began, and when she heard about the carnage at the shipyard she set out to find Grandpa and Andrew, who were both working there. She expected the worst when she saw the badly blasted Neptune Bar on the other side of York Street, but Granda, who regularly repaired there for his daily refreshment, had not been present. Both he and my uncle Andrew, who was a ship's plater, were safe, but it was a tragic day for many, and the city mourned the victims.

German U-boats continued to send thousands of tons of our merchant shipping to the bottom. Rationing became stricter still, and familiar things all but disappeared from the home menus of this beleaguered nation. No longer did we have Corn Flakes; instead we had Wheat Flakes, and we believed what the Ministry of Food told us about their being good for us. Instead of Stork Margarine there was a National Margarine which tasted like lard, but was good for pastry making if any could be spared. In England, with its warmer climate, there was a glut of fruit on the trees, but with the war-time system of priorities it could not be transported to Scotland, and so for us fruit more or less disappeared. Because of the scarcity of sugar for jam-making, much of it was in fact left to rot. Anything involving sugar was out of the question unless a few pounds could be saved by, for instance, doing without sugar in tea. In such cases, a pinch of salt would help to take away the tea's bitter taste – or so it was said!

Our amusements were as simple as ever, if not more so. Sometimes of a Sunday, my chum Peggy, Wull, Bill and I would go for a walk, and I remember our once walking to the Shakkin' Briggie at Cults, taking a route from the back of Kaimhill, along what was then quite a spectacular country road lined with trees thick in their summer foliage. The lads pointed to a large house situated in its own grounds, which they said belonged to their Officer in the 8th Battalion Gordon Highlanders. He was, I think, their C.O. (Company Officer), and they referred to him as Cecil. This was Henry Cecil, who lived in the big house with his wife and small son. The lads described him as a very tall man, whom they liked – and a popular Officer was indeed a rarity. Much later in the war, Henry Cecil was killed in North Africa. His widow eventually married Boyd Rochfort, the race horse owner and trainer, and the son of her first marriage is often seen on television at race meetings in that same capacity.

In town one day, Bill decided to take a bus to Fittie and visit my grandmother, with whom he got on very well. Standing at the bus stop, he waited in vain for any bus that said 'Fittie' on the front. It was not until he asked someone in the queue that he discovered that 'Footdee' was the word to look for. On another occasion, a dreich rainy day, Bill chanced to meet my grandmother in George Street. After they had stood talking a while, my Granny offered Bill her umbrella, as she was about to go home and it would be a shame to have his uniform soaked in the downpour. Not one to take 'no' for an answer, she was quite adamant that Bill should borrow her umbrella, under which they had been standing, and Bill had to make good his escape as best he could. What a picture it would have made – a soldier in the Gordons walking around with a red 'chubby'! We fell about laughing when Bill told us; his comment on the matter was what we already knew, that my grandmother was 'a very determined lady'.

Soldiers were by this time stationed in schools, halls, churches – all over the place, in addition to their main quarters at the Gordon Barracks, so that in addition to the usual square-bashing at the Barracks it was common to see men out on Physical Training, dressed in black shorts, white vests, socks and black 'jimmies'. Out on the streets they ran, accompanied by a loud Sergeant or PT Instructor and wishing no doubt that they were back in their billets with a cup of tea, a rowie and a smoke. Bill and Wullie were still billeted in Skene Square School. On Riverside Drive, next to the Dee, they marched in full uniform complete with respirators and other gear, drilling, wheeling and turning with much stamping of feet in heavy army boots, and with much bawling and shouting as the army turned these raw recruits into part of the British fighting machine. They could be seen on route marches, also in full gear, stepping out smartly in unison under the eagle eye of their Sergeant as they whistled the tune of 'Colonel Bogey' or sang at the tops of their voices a certain set of rude verses, which brought giggles from the girls among the waving bystanders.

Even in the worst years of the war, life for girls of my age could be interesting, often entertaining, and sometimes quite romantic, even if this romance existed only in our minds, conjured up by the sight of so many young men in khaki and Navy or Air Force blue. As I mentioned earlier, airmen were nicknamed the 'Brylcreem Boys', slicked-down, shiny hair being still very fashionable at that time. Apart from the husband of our next-door neighbour, Chrissie Wilson, I never knew many members of that particular branch of the Armed Forces. Also known as 'The Glamour Boys', they were reputed to talk in a slang of their own, always 'shooting a line' or 'pranging a plane', with everything being 'a piece of cake', but I suspect this to have been the preserve of the officer class rather than the ACI. Those Spitfire and Hurricane crews were soon to play their own magnificent part in a war that was fought in the skies as much as it was on land or sea.

CHAPTER 5

On 7 September 1940, the 'phoney war' was brought well and truly to an end. The German Luftwaffe, which had so far confined its activities to raiding RAF bases, launched its Blitzkreig ('lightning war') against London, raining bombs on the Dockland and City areas, which burned like a bonfire. Spitfires and Hurricanes from Kent, manned by young pilots just like the lads we knew, shot down many enemy planes on this and innumerable other mass raids, but two thousand civilians were killed or maimed in the course of Hitler's attempts to destroy London. By crippling major cities, terrorising their populations and wrecking morale, he hoped to make easy his next step, 'Operation Sealion', the invasion of Britain by sea. Other cities in England also therefore took the brunt of the bombing and the centre of Coventry was razed to the ground, but through it all came the voice of Winston Churchill (who would not even pay the Germans the courtesy of pronouncing their words properly) affirming that Britain would never surrender to the 'Nazzies'. The battle in the skies raged for days at a time, until eventually the bravery of 'The Few' thwarted Hitler's intentions. His so-called lightning war failed, and Operation Sealion was postponed.

Along came another rash of rules and regulations – 'Use less fuel', 'Only five inches of bath water to be used', etc. In warmer weather, women and girls were urged to wear ankle socks in order to save scarce stocking material. Some coloured their legs with cold tea or cocoa to simulate stockings, painting on a 'seam' with marker pen or pencil. Considerable skill could be developed at this, although the help of someone with a steady hand was required to put in the 'seam' and (even better) to draw a nicely-shaped 'heel' as found on the best-quality garments. In keeping with the times, hair styles became simpler, except for when we went dancing, at which times the curling tongs or hair curlers came into play. It was at this time that the 'Dinkie' hair curler came on the market, making hair setting much easier. Most of the time we simply tied narrow bands of thin cloth round our heads then tucked our hair into that. Sometimes a wider piece of cloth would be used to make a bandau (or bandana), which became standard in factories and other places where safety at machines was essential. Often an old silk stocking, laddered and sewn too many times to be worn, was used in place of the cloth.

'Make-do and mend' was the order of the day, although this was nothing new to the many who had been doing little else since the onset of the Depression in 1929-1930, and had long been used to having to deny themselves the finer things in life. There was now more work to be had, especially in ship-building, coal-mining and steel-making for the war effort, and while wages were still small, overtime could considerably increase the size of one's pay packet.

Many of the household goods on which that pay might have been spent had, however, become either scarce or unobtainable. Carpets and wallpapers were in very short supply, so the inventive householder had to improvise with such techniques as the stippling that I have already described. For blankets, surplus pieces of knitting would be pulled apart and the wool recycled to become crocheted squares which would be joined together. With our bigger house and the growing size of our family, more beds and bedding were required, which did not make our financial situation any easier. Although we had our three coal fires plus a back-to-back grate in the small kitchen, we were never able to light them all, so priority was given to the fires in the front and upstairs back bedrooms in order to keep the rooms aired, but even then they could only be lit occasionally. Once again we found ourselves facing winter, the icy pictures on our windows never melting from October onwards, but still we could count ourselves lucky. Unlike those who still lived in the old, cramped houses with no inside toilets or hot water, we could sit cosily by our living-room fire, the heat from which travelled through the back-to-back grate and helped to warm the kitchen (always called 'scullery' in Aberdeen in those days). A kettle of water was always kept on the hob, and the oven doubled as a dryer of kindling sticks and heater of socks and jerseys on cold mornings. Cooking was done on the gas cooker, the large oven of which was used for the baking. A whistling kettle sat ready for use, and a coffee pot was at hand to heat and reheat precious grounds. None of us would drink reheated tea, so we eked out our rations in this way.

We never heard weather forecasts. These were kept rather hush-hush, although it hardly seemed to matter, as nothing stopped the Luftwaffe from carrying out its heavy bombing raids on London and the Home Counties night after dark night, with our RAF fighters unable to spot them as they had done in the September daylight raids. Most of our armament factories and naval bases were situated in England, but with the proximity of Hitler's air bases in Norway, Glasgow and Belfast also suffered air attacks. While Aberdeen had its share of raids, which were bad enough, in England casualties amounted to thousands, and it seemed that the sirens would never stop.

Our two soldiers Bill and Wullie were moved with their battalion to Belhelvie, not too far away, so that when the army condescended to give them a 12 hour pass they came to our house as usual and were able to enjoy some home comforts. One night Bill came alone and we went to the pictures. He missed the bus back to camp, but, not too dismayed, borrowed a small bicycle belonging to my younger brother John. Off he set for Belhelvie, his knees touching the handlebars. Air-raid sirens wailed as he neared the top of Market Street, but he pedalled on. A bomb hit a bank in Market Street and he was nearly lifted off the cassies ('blown nearly on to King Street', he said later), but he remained unscathed. He was nearly at camp when a policeman stopped him and in a broad Buchan voice enquired, 'Ye ken ye hivna got a light on yer bike?' Suitably admonished, Bill carried on to his destination.

At work, we heard on the grapevine one day that a visit by King George VI and Queen Elizabeth was taking place at the docks. On Albert Quay the sailors were lined up in their 'Tiddly' (their best number ones) and inspecting them were the two Royals. The King in Admiral's uniform and the Queen, smiling and nodding, were watched avidly by the small crowd, in which were all the girls from our now-deserted place of work. The Queen looked small and dainty in a halo hat, smooth-textured fur coat and fashionable high-heeled shoes. We were so excited when we got back to work; for the first time we had seen the King and Queen in person!

That Hogmanay, the Reid family next door had a party, to which we younger ones were invited. Mrs Reid sat looking plump and happy as we all trooped in knowing as she did that her daughters would be doing all the necessary entertaining. Gladys Reid, her natural blonde hair worn shoulder length, had her Dutch soldier with her, an affable lad in uniform with the 'Free Dutch' flash on his shoulder. Finding his name unpronounce-able, we just called him Bert. He was very much looking forward to a Scottish Hogmanay.

Winnie, Mrs Reid's youngest daughter, had with her a Free Czech air-man in Air Force blue. We were told to call him Josef. He was tall and good looking but rather quiet and shy, perhaps because he did not under-stand much of the conversation going on around him. We felt sympathy for these lads, knowing that their homeland was occupied by Hitler's ar-mies. Thoughts of their families must have been in their minds as another New Year dawned, far from home in a long war. Bill, in his Army uni-form, kept the party lively with his accordion. He had come all the way from Huntly where he was now stationed, the Battalion having been moved again. Bert, our Dutchman, loved the Scottish dance music and asked Bill again and again to play 'Lock Lomond'. He couldn't get the 'och' part at all, so 'Lock Lomond' it had to be until the gramophone started up with all the latest records. Gladys' favourite, 'Begin the Beguine', was among them, of course, and we sang all the silly songs like 'Mairzy Doats and Dozy Doats', and all the other favourites of the time.

Josef, Winnie and I took a trip into town on the tramcar as Winnie wanted my opinion on the choice of a skirt and blouse from 'E and M's'. Josef had given her money to buy them for her birthday, and as we girls could never afford to buy things from such an up-market shop, the prospect was quite exciting. Winnie settled on a dusky pink wool skirt and a multi-coloured silk blouse. Upstairs on the tram home, she showed Josef her purchase, and he didn't like it. 'You be like a geepsy!' This quiet, rather elegant airman had taste! Later, Gladys married Bert and Winnie married Josef, with whom she went to live in Prague after the war.

In our household we had a cat – a pet which we seemed constantly to be lifting from easychairs when somebody wanted to sit down. She was a small, quiet, insignificant black and white creature, neutered, as my mother didn't relish the idea of 'kitlins', as she called them. Our little moggy didn't go out much at all, preferring her customary spot by the fireplace. One dark night the sirens went and incendiaries were dropped, causing a conflagration somewhere on the north side of the city. Carefully, to avoid showing any light, we opened the front door to have a look. Something furry went scurrying past my feet; it turned out to be a very beautiful but very scared marmalade cat with pale orange striped fur and deep green eyes. Where she came from nobody knew, but with a very haughty look at our own very ordinary cat she began a round of various lodgings in our neighbours' houses, fed by everyone and giving allegiance to no-one in particular. This cat was there to stay, it seemed, so she had to have a name, preferably one suitable for a feline who was no ordinary moggy. Mrs Stewart's young son christened her 'Tara Wara, the tartan cat', adding, 'Of no fixed abode'. Very apt, we all thought, and so 'Tara' it was. Time passed and it was noted that Tara was becoming rather fat. Certain conclusions were drawn, but in whose house the happy event would occur was anyone's guess. The answer came one morning when Mrs Wilson rushed in and announced, 'Tara's had kittens in the bottom of my wardrobe!' We all promptly heaved a sigh of relief.

By 1941, the war was having a swingeing effect on people's lives. Conscription of both men and women was relentless, and married women who had previously followed the traditional pattern of staying at home and having children now found a ready market for their labour, replacing men as bus and tram conductresses, in jobs on the railways, and as workers in munitions factories. The Government made available creche facilities to woo back to work these young women who, with the memory of the Depression years still fresh, were not slow to take the opportunity of earning money. Previously, even when work was available it had often been subject to the sanction 'No Married Women Need Apply', which added to the general hardship, especially if the recognised family breadwinners were unemployed. The wages paid to conscripted married men were very small, and couples found themselves having to make use of the 'never-never' while having very little income with which to pay it off. A job for the wife, in the knowledge that only single girls would be called into the Forces, was therefore a godsend.

In winter, Huntly where the 8th Gordons were stationed was by all accounts a bleak place. 'Out in the wilds', the two lads said, but then the terrain was very suitable for the hard slog of training and hardening for battle. Ploughing through slush and snow on route marches and manoeuvres, queuing in the cold for breakfast in the early dawn after reveille, the constant 'bull' of keeping uniform, boots and webbing spotlessly clean – this was daily life for the tough, enduring men of the Scottish regiments. Not that all of the men were actually Scottish; some English lads slogged it out alongside their Scottish comrades, and one day Bill brought to our house a soldier from London. Over a cup of tea, he remarked how much he admired our red-tiled houses at Kaimhill. 'Like a little toy town' was how he described them. Much later in the war, I was saddened to hear that this tall, likeable lad had been killed in North Africa, but there were to be sad times for many of us before the conflict was over.

It seems that quite a number of local lads were stationed at Huntly, and like Bill and Wull they came into town when a 12 hour pass was granted. This meant being back at camp in time for reveille at 6 a.m. the following day, so after a picture show, a dance or whatever, they would have a few hours' sleep then go to the station and catch a train at about 4 a.m. Bill and Wull would tramp through the snow all the way from Kaimhill, then, with the other soldiers, would collapse into a train compartment and promptly fall asleep. At the other end, the voice of the station porter calling 'Huntly' would rouse them from their slumbers, and, bleary-eyed, they would tumble out in some confusion on to the platform. One morning it all came close to going disastrously wrong. Someone heard what they thought was the shout of 'Huntly', and in their usual dazed state the lads scrambled out only to find themselves on the station platform at Gartly. There was a mad rush back on to the train; 'Well', they said a little sheepishly afterwards, 'it sounded like Huntly!'

The man who wrote the song 'Yes, We Have No Bananas' cannot have known how true his words were to become, as we had no fruit at all by 1941. Potatoes, however, were not rationed, so many a weird and wonderful dish was concocted with these and the ubiquitous dried egg. My Aunt Daisy would make whipped cream by mixing custard with dried milk then gently folding it into creamed margarine, with delicious results.

By Government order, a large contingent of girls at Enterprise Stores, myself included, was taken away from braiding fish nets and was instructed in the making of camouflage nets. These were easier to deal with, but to earn our weekly wage, which stood unchanged at 30 shillings (no mean sum in those days) we had to produce a larger number - eight to ten a week, I seem to remember. There was therefore no time to be idle.

One morning at work I developed a severe toothache, and during my dinner hour I went to a dentist in Victoria Road, Torry. This was an excellent man by the name of Mr E G Hazel. He seated me in the dreaded chair, which faced a large bay window, and put an injection in the area of the offending back teeth. With a cheery smile, he then left me for a few minutes while he finished his dinner. The sirens had sounded and gunfire could be heard. Through the window I watched Spitfires chasing an enemy plane, and this at least took my mind off my now 'frozen' teeth. Back came the dentist, who quickly and calmly got to work, and in seconds the offending teeth were out, with no pain or discomfort at all. On that day I lost any fear of dentists; he was the best. His fee – 2s. 6d. (12 pence)!

In time-honoured fashion, my friend Peggy and I continued to 'walk the mat' on Sunday evenings. For Saturday night dancing, we bought new Tangee lipstick from Woolworths, which was unique in giving a natural colour instead of the usual intense reds. We wore comparatively little make-up, just a spot of vanishing cream and our Tangee, with certainly no blusher (or 'rouge', as it was simply known then). We had youth on our side, and even if our naturally coloured cheeks became a little rosy during the dancing, that could quickly be remedied with a touch of face powder.

The cinema was as potent a form of escapism as ever, not so much now from poverty and poor surroundings as from the austerity and uncertainty of the times that had come upon us. American musicals were very popular everywhere, their songs and lavish scenery providing just the tonic that was needed in black-out Britain. 'Blue skies around the corner', went one popular number, and we believed it.

'Somebody's smoking Pasha!' One luxury that had previously been taken for granted but which had now more or less gone 'under the counter' for the general public was the cigarette. Anyone managing to obtain a packet of ten would find that it contained eight with standard Virginia tobacco, plus two Pasha, which when smoked had a very distinctive and easily discernible smell. I don't know where they came from (some said India), but the aroma that they produced was not particularly pleasant, and often when sitting in the cinema one's nose would be assailed when somebody close by lit one. At that point, some comic (and there always was one) would say loudly, 'Somebody's smoking Pasha!', and there would be laughter in the immediate area. People were tolerant, and any cause for laughter was always welcome.

From Huntly, some of the Eighth Battalion Gordon Highlanders were moved in the course of 1941 to Peterculter, then little more than a pleasant, quiet village on the banks of the Dee, with picturesque views in its surrounding countryside, and with its famous statue of Rob Roy where he is reputed to have leapt the river. Employment in the village was centred chiefly at the paper mill, whose workers lived in the houses nearby.

Private billets were obtained for the soldiers by Government order. Anyone with a spare room was required, in return for a few shillings per week, to house a member of the Army, and in this way many long-lasting friendships were formed. Dances were held at the local hotel, the Gordon Arms, and many a good evening we had there in the company of friends, especially the McDonald family, whose daughter Margaret, a very pretty fair-haired girl, sometimes invited me to stay overnight. The McDonalds were warm-hearted people who shared their meals as generously with us as they did with their billettees, among whom was Wull. When Wull's parents, Mr and Mrs Young, came to visit us at Kaimhill, they made a point of visiting the McDonalds to thank them for being so good to their only son.

At Fittie one dinner time, my Grandmother offered me, as was her custom, a 'suppie soup', which with a piece of bread was the usual dinner-time fare. During the ensuing conversation, she asked about Bill, with whom I had been keeping company for some time, although I never forsook my chum Peggy until she was later conscripted to the Women's Auxiliary Air Force (the WAAF). 'Oh', I replied airily, 'I've fallen out with him – I dinna want a steady boyfriend'. At this, Granny, the matriarch of the family, made her displeasure felt in no uncertain terms. 'A fine boy, disna drink', etc, etc – on she went, but I was adamant. Finally came an ultimatum. 'Ye've fa'n oot, so ye'd better fa' in again, or ye dinna come back for yer dinner!' Walking back to work with the Fittie girls, I gave them a blow-by-blow account of this stramash, which they thought quite comical. The situation was resolved when Bill, who had been away on leave at his Lanarkshire home, arrived at our door carrying a peace-offering which he presented to my mother. It was a large chicken, the welcome extended to which was more or less equal to that extended to Bill himself. We went to the pictures that night, and I went back to Granny's for my 'suppie soup'.

On the Home Front (as it was now called), 1941 brought many changes and innovations, but few as marked as the arrival in our midst of a Morrison Shelter. Named after Herbert Morrison, M.P., these massive structures were designed to give protection to families whose gardens were too small for an Anderson Shelter, and every house in our district was offered one. Slightly larger than a double bed, the Morrison Shelter consisted of four steel posts four feet in height, supporting a roof of solid steel, and was sprung like a bed at floor level. In the event of a raid, we were all expected to pile into it. It would, we were informed, withstand anything short of a direct hit; comforted with that thought, the family all had a try at lying or sitting in it, the younger ones eager for a shottie in this strange contraption of whose real purpose they were mercifully unaware.

'Is that one of ours or one of theirs?', my little sister Eleanor, not yet school age, would ask when we heard bombers at night. Even children could tell the difference in the engines' sound, and all too often it was 'one of theirs'. Initially, our Morrison shelter had pride of place in our living room, but not for long. It took up a lot of space, and, showing distinct signs of disenchantment with it, my mother decided that it should be moved to the front room, which was used as a lounge or as a bedroom, depending on Mother's mood. As ever, there was method in this, as the addition of mattresses inside and on the top turned the shelter into a useful bunk bed with which to accommodate the guests that so often stayed with us, but this idea did not last either. Putting a mattress on top was all right, but for safety reasons the covering of the wire springing in the bottom of the shelter was not advised. After a few air-raid scares we found that we could not all get into it, but it did afford us some sense of security, and for additional shelter we could always retreat to the cupboard under the stairs, owl lamp and all.

Failing to wipe out the RAF, Hitler turned East to invade Russia, which he saw as the greater menace. The attack began in June 1941, and from then on it was Fascist against Communist. Against that historic background, my work at the docks came to an end. We had completed our quota of camouflage nets, and with so many fishing boats having been taken over for war duties there was now far less of a requirement for fishing nets. Most of the younger girls such as myself were therefore paid off, leaving only the older, more experienced women to continue net-making. I was sorry to leave the happy atmosphere of Enterprise Stores, the friendly girls, Jimmy our kind foreman, the songs, the jokes and the danger that we had all shared. We would all miss the friendly waves and greetings from the anti-aircraft gunners on the quay and the 'Good morning, girls!' from the minesweeper crews in the basin, but I was lucky. My stint as a Saturday girl in the George Street Woolworth's worked in my favour, as I was immediately taken on again. We were all required to go through the interview with the Staff Supervisor, adding up columns of figures, etc, but I was an 'old hand'. So back I went to begin with the new girls on the following Monday morning at 9 a.m. Woolies were by this time losing far more employees to the Forces, as single girls were being conscripted, and no doubt for that reason there was now getting to be quite a number of married women on the staff.

Founded in New York by Frank Whitfield away back in 1879, Woolworths was the first concern of its kind – a 5 and 10 cent store. In Britain it was the 'nothing over sixpence' store, and it was a great institution in every city, giving value for money on such a variety of goods that its aisles were always thronged. In Aberdeen a 'walkie roon' Woolies' was as essential as 'a rakie roon' the Castler' on a Friday.

My working hours were much longer than they had been at the net braiding, and although the work was pleasant, there seemed to be many long hours between 9 in the morning and the time when we could finally pitch out through the maze of ARP baffle walls and sandbags and into the street at the end of the day. At 9 o'clock prompt we were behind our allotted counters, waiting for the ringing of the bell which signalled that the cash registers could be opened and the float deposited. From then until our staggered lunch breaks we were kept fully occupied. On Mondays and Fridays, the closing bell rang at 7 p.m., while on Thursdays it was 8 p.m. and on Saturdays it was 9. On Wednesdays we closed at 1 p.m. for our half-day.

Just as before, I wore the pocketless plum-coloured uniform with the letter W embroidered in gold on its lapels, and just as before our coats and handbags were locked away in a cloakroom, the key to which was in the charge of one of the Staff Supervisors, an amiable middle-aged lady who had a good rapport with the girls while still keeping them at a repectful distance. Our Assistant Manager and floor walker was a very tall man named Mr France. Equipped with eyes like a hawk, he could spot a mistake in a cash till, such as the giving out of wrong change, from the middle of a crowded shop. He soon disappeared (into the forces, I seem to remember) and his replacement was a Miss Logan. A middle-aged spinster, this lady looked severe indeed, with sharp features and tightly drawn-back hair. This together with her air of efficiency, which was typical of Woolworths' staff management, made her seem quite a formidable figure. The Manager, whose name I cannot recall, was a Welshman with whom I did not always get on well, although of course he was there to keep everyone in line, and no-one who is in such a position is likely to enjoy much popularity!

Over the day, the latest records were played from the music counter, and so we often worked to our favourite dance tunes – 'Little Sir Echo', 'Bless 'Em All', 'Kiss Me Goodnight Sergeant Major', and many others. Vera Lynne's popularity never waned, her voice reaching out to every corner of the battle zones in what was becoming truly a World War. There were always members of the armed forces in the shop buying such things as shaving soap and writing paper, and sometimes one of these lads would take a fancy to one of the girls and ask for a date. Many a romance began in this way.

At home, meanwhile, Grandmother Masson was very excited about the war between Germany and Russia. Every other day she came all the way to Kaimhill from Fittie – 'Nae enough t' dae there!' When she wasn't at our house she walked to Aunt Daisy's, something that she and I had often done during my childhood. Sometimes she would bring the younger children sweeties in a little bag, saying as she handed them out

'Smackery isna good for ye!' Over the usual fly-cup she would regale everyone with her version of the names of Russian cities taken as the Germans advanced, and would read pieces from her daily paper. 'Wait till the afa' Russian winter comes', she said knowingly, and she was right. When the severe winter weather did come on the Eastern Front, both sides became completely bogged down and the Germans, who were not equipped for such conditions, suffered so many casualties from the freezing cold that they could not go on.

We received all our Fittie news from Granny, living as she did in the house in which Granda was born and which still had on its door the nameplate of his father, William Masson, Ship's Pilot, for whom it was built. Granda so loved the sea that he wouldn't budge from beside it. Once when he and Granny were invited out tò the country he dug his heels in and announced that he wasn't going. But he didn't dig them in far enough, and soon he was on his way out of town with Granny in the little old car belonging to my young uncle Andrew, of whom I wrote in my previous book *A Time Of Our Lives*. Andrew was married by this time and had two young children. The family lived in the city centre, Andrew, as a ship's plater in Hall Russell's, being in a reserved occupation.

The bombing raids on Aberdeen prompted Andrew to build a small chalet in the country, not far away from town, and there the family lived during the summer. Later, with the help of my young brother John, he added a fireplace in which wood, of which there was plenty lying around, could be burned for heating. Andrew, it must be said, was a genius at utilising bits and pieces that others might simply throw out. He was always on the lookout for the oddest items, which he would cleverly convert into something useful. Cocky Hunter's was his favourite haunt, and it was there that he found a brass canopy and some tiles to give the fireplace (as he put it) 'a touch of class' – and all for only a bob.

The gramophone was also brought on that trip to the country, but was soon on its way back. Granda, fed up at not having his daily walk on the beach and, more importantly, his bottle of beer at the Neptune, went out looking for a hostelry. He didn't find one. Instead, he got lost in a maze of hedges and fell asleep on the grassy verge where Andrew found him. After that he decided that he had had enough of the country. 'Na, na, it's nae for me', he said, 'too far fae the beach!' I must admit that I shared this sentiment. The country was all right for a picnic, but my childhood roots were by the sea. Similarly, a trip to the Duthie Park or to Hazlehead Park was fine, but Fittie had been my world. Walking along the beach almost every Sunday, summer and winter, with my chum Dorothy Gordon from St Clements Street; watching the big waves at high tide and running up the 'slippies' as a particularly large wave came rolling in towards us, crashing on the bottom of the slip and showering us with spray; walking along the North Pier and watching the old 'smoky Joe' trawlers as they crossed the bar and headed out into the bay, ploughing through the troughs of the North Sea – that was my background, and these had still been the child-like pleasures of myself and my young friends when we were 13 or 14. We weren't called 'teenagers' in those days; we were the 'young eens', or the 'young quines and the young loons', and despite the terrible effects of the Depression in the 1930s we retained the pleasures of childhood for much longer than is possible nowadays. It was, as I remarked in *A Time Of Our Lives*, a precious innocence, and it carried us right though until the time that the world went to war and most of my generation became caught up in the conflict.

I said that many a romance began over the counters at Woolworths. Indeed, a few marriage matches resulted. For the honeymoon, the bride would take her annual paid holidays of just one week, while the bride-groom would be granted the seven days' leave of honeymoon to which he was entitled if stationed in the UK. I used to feel sorry for the service-men who, three or four months later, would be given another week's leave while their wives had to work because the money was so badly needed. I remember how one girl, who worked at the kitchen-ware counter, was able to see her new husband four or five times a day when he came in and out of the shop, but prolonged talk was not encouraged, and they had to be careful.

There came a day when the Government ordered the removal of all metal fencing and railings that could be safely and legally taken, to be melted down for armaments. It was also decreed that paper was to be conserved, and so Woolworths immediately stopped issuing paper bags for purchases. At the time, I was working at the hardware counter, at which we sold a multitude of items, including nails and screws. A man asked for 'Two pun' o' nails'; I weighed them out and asked him if he had a bag to put them in. Puzzled, he looked at me and asked why no bag. I duly explained, and he went away with 'two pun' o' nails' in the large patch pockets of his overcoat!

There appeared on the canteen wall a notice proclaiming that staff must now take turns at firewatching duties. A rota was drawn up assigning two firewatchers at a time to spend the night in the building, dealing quickly with any incendiary bombs that might land there. In the small room that we called the canteen, two folding beds with pillows and blankets were set up. We were given a stirrup pump, a bucket of sand, and water pails painted red with 'ARP' in black on them. This, I gather, was standard equipment in city centre buildings.

I found my name on the rota, and to my dismay my partner on my first stint was to be none other than Miss Logan! I quaked at the thought of spending all these hours with such a personage, but was pleasantly surprised to find her a most interesting and pleasant companion. We talked, drank tea, read books and laughed as she told me of some hilarious moments in her career with Woolworths. Next day, I was able to tell the girls that our Assistant Manageress was 'affa fine company', but I don't think they really believed me!

Of all the goods that were now in very short supply, the most problematic for us was without doubt steel wool. We were constantly asked for it, but had to tell customers, 'Sorry, we don't have any'. They would answer, 'Well, you used to have it', with the emphasis on the 'used', and with a rather accusing look. To this we would blithely reply, 'Remember, there's a war on!'. Usually we got away with it; one irate customer did report us to the manager for being cheeky, which brought a reprimand, but it didn't stop us, and often this our standard response would be accompanied by a fit of giggling which necessitated a quick disappearance from view behind the counter.

I was tidying and laying out the stock on my counter one day when a friendly, familiar voice said, 'Hello, Ethel'. A very handsome RAF officer stood before me. It was Joe Lamont, brother of my chum Nan with whom I had worked in the oatcake factory. Joe told me that he had been in Canada for some months, training to be a navigator. He had an emblem half-wing denoting this. We spoke for a short time, recalling the picnics that we had had with the large Lamont family, the evenings when he walked me from his home to the Astoria for my halfpenny tram journey to Woodside, and the day when, as a railway steward of seventeen, he took Nan and myself on a train trip to Elgin. Soon he had to go; his leave had ended and he was returning to his Bomber Squadron in England. I never saw him again. His plane was shot down over Germany, and the entire crew died. Much later, I heard from a member of the Lamont family that his mother, although she lived into old age, never came to terms with her loss.

On the War Memorial at Fittie is the name John Mauchline, Stoker MN (Merchant Navy). As I related in *A Time Of Our Lives*, he and I were brought up together in Links Street, playing 'hoosies' in the Copie doorway with the other kids in those happier times. One day, I met Johnny and his cousin Charles in the shop. Aged all of 18, they were with the convoys that sailed through the bitter North Atlantic, carrying armaments to Russia for use against the Nazis. They too died when their ship was sunk, and I was to hear of many others of my generation who ended their pilgrimage on earth in the cause of war.

But life went on, and new life was created. An eighth child arrived in our family. My mother was not yet 40 years old, and I admit that I initially felt very resentful of this new drain on our financial resources. But then many people's finances were stretched, the better-off seeming to get richer while the rest merely got by. We still always had food on the table – lots of fish as usual, and the arrival of my new baby sister, Wilma, made little difference to that. New nappies were bought and yet another pram – a utility model of a kind just recently introduced. During the last few months of my mother's pregnancy, I had to spend my Wednesday half-day not at the Palais but at the kitchen sink, doing the family washing. Hard work it was too, with the only labour-saving device our pre-war Acme wringer. I felt sorry for my mother, who often felt unwell, but women had little choice in these matters at that time. Contraceptives were on the market, but as one woman that I remember so succinctly remarked, 'Ye can lead a horse to water but ye canna mak' it drink!'

Only on completion of an afternoon's hard work could I go off to the pictures with Bill, and there was plenty more hard work to come, as when our new baby sister was born in Foresterhill Hospital, Granny came to take over the household. The month was November and the weather was cold– almost as cold as the reception that she gave to our sitting down for too long after work. Domestic chores had to be shared, and no idle hands were allowed. It came as quite a relief when our industrious Grandmother eventually returned to the sanctuary of her own home in Fittie.

On 7 December 1941, Japan attacked the American Navy at Pearl Harbour in the Pacific, destroying many of the (rather ancient) ships in the harbour. At that, America mobilised, and the long-felt effects of the great Depression were brought to an end as people went to work to aid a war which America had so long resisted entering. Soon American troops were 'overpaid, oversexed, and over here', and the destinies of millions of people were in the hands of the three Allied leaders, Winston Churchill, Franklin D. Roosevelt and Joseph Stalin.

At home that fateful day, my mother, stoic and resilient as always, was cooking supper for the large family – fish soup, as my father was home from sea with his usual bass bag. Father was catching up on sleep before taking my mother to the Tivoli Theatre that night, as he had only 48 hours ashore before returning to the hard grind and constant danger of his work at sea. Grandmother Masson, sitting at our table with her cup of tea and 'fine piece', would glower at him as he came in from the Bridge of Dee Bar and would make tut-tutting noises, but father would always see that she had some fish to take home with her, and a half-crown to give to Granda for a pint in the Neptune!

As the tempo of the war increased, so did the number of weddings. Banns were called from church steps if time was short for men who, home on a 48 hour pass, decided to tie the knot before being shipped out. The time of square-bashing and hard training was over for them, but conscription meant a steady flow of new recruits in the frantic fight against first the Axis powers and now the Japanese as well. The Commandos did their training in the bleakest areas of Scotland during the coldest weather that the Highlands could offer. A special 'crack' unit, they were brave and tough men, as were all those who fought in the Scottish regiments.

In the Ross household, the eldest daughter Margaret had said her good-byes to her soldier husband. They had been married only a short time, and she was very despondent when, his embarkation leave over, he set sail for the Far East along with thousands of other soldiers in their crowded troopships. Those at home were not told where the ships were bound, but it was Singapore.

In the Wilson family, the husband of their eldest daughter Nettie had been in the Middle East for some time with General Auchinleck's army, which was now retreating after success followed by failure against the might of Rommel's Panzers in the fight for Middle East oil. Erwin Rommel, Commander of Hitler's Afrika Korps, and nicknamed 'the Desert Fox', had driven the British back to within 60 miles of Alexandria, and things were looking very bleak.

Most of our neighbours' houses in Kaimhill were very crowded, the young unmarried members of the family having to remain at home as there was no accommodation elsewhere. With luxuries unaffordable or unobtainable, people just had to 'make do' – a term frequently heard during the war. Many, like my own family, had moved from small tenement rooms to those nice terraced houses in 1939 or 1940, and few had much in the way of furniture or carpets. Wages had not increased much, not in the North-East anyway, and life could be a struggle.

But Bill and I had just become engaged! Proudly, I showed off the ring to my colleagues at Woolworth's. Bill had gone to his home in Lanark-shire on Army leave, and I had taken a couple of days off work to meet him in Glasgow. Arriving on the train, it then took a bus journey and what seemed a very long walk up a country road before we reached the small-holding that was his home. It seemed a lonely place, set against a background of distant pit bings that proclaimed this to be a mining community as well as a farming one. Bill's large family seemed a little non-plussed at my Aberdeen accent, which they had never heard before, but I could understand their broad Lanarkshire quite well, as my father was born near Glasgow and I had also become quite used to the Glasgow brogue of Bill's pal Wullie Young.

For all the distance and differences separating them, our families had become very close. My parents had been very good to the lads and to their relatives who arrived on the doorstep from time to time. My father often booked seats at the Tivoli Theatre for the lads, knowing that their army pay would not stretch to such things. Wullie, meanwhile, would come to our door bearing generous food parcels from home when he returned from leave.

However, by late 1941 the lads' time in local camps was drawing to an end. Following the replacement of the army's existing six-pound anti-tankshell guns with new seventeen-pounders, part of the Gordons regiment was to be trained for anti-tank duties, and so that winter off the two went to Norfolk. There, 'somewhere in England', or, to be more precise, on a muddy, sodden farmer's field one night, they hauled this great gun after a heavy day's training. Soaked in the cold heavy rain, they were pulling and pushing the wretched thing over the miry earth when the irate farmer appeared, reviling the b!?*!* Army and its b!?*!* gun for the mess it had made of his field, and ordering all concerned off his property. But this was the British Army and this was war time; the episode ended with hot soup in the farm kitchen and a dry bed for the lads in the large barn!

Before long, the whole of Southern England (particularly Devon and Cornwall) would see platoons of young, homesick, bewildered American soldiers surveying this bleak, drizzly land as they commenced their training so far from home. They would bring with them their own comforts, such as the PX, which was their equivalent of the British NAAFI, except that it sold ice cream-flavour chewing gum, good American coffee and doughnuts to dunk in it, Spam, American cigarettes, nylons, blueberry pie and many other things dear to the Transatlantic heart. They had hot showers in their camps, well-cut fine green khaki uniforms with cheese-cutter caps and brown leather shoes, and they wore collar and tie with their dress uniform. With them would come the Jitterbug, replacing the Palais Glide and the Lambeth Walk in our dance halls, while on the radio the American Forces Network brought the tunes of the Glenn Miller orchestra – 'Little Brown Jug', 'Moonlight Serenade', 'Pennsylvania 65000', 'In the Mood', 'Chattanooga Choo-Choo' In their smart uniforms, American drawl, sloppy salute and all, these lads would win some hearts and break many more.

Wedding day, 31 January 1942

CHAPTER 6

'Absence makes the heart grow fonder', as the old saying goes. It was certainly true in the case of Bill and myself, and I looked forward to his next leave at the end of January 1942 when we would be married. I still had my chums at work, with whom I went to the pictures and to dances, but soon I would have to start preparations for my wedding. I planned to wear a suit and one of the rather frivolous hats which were in vogue at the time, but in the end it was a white wedding, involving a great deal more work and expense for an already very busy household. Invitations for both families' relatives were printed, and although, in retrospect, a quieter wedding might have been wiser, my mother declared, 'You're the eldest and the first to be married, so a white wedding's best!'

When at last the time came, Bill had to travel all the way from Norfolk, a long and tedious journey on a packed train whose corridors were jammed with servicemen. Most of them lay asleep, heads on kitbags and their gear filling every available space so that a trip to the toilet became a somewhat hazardous affair, occasioning groans and sleepy complaints from the recumbent figures. A change of train at York was necessary, then another at Edinburgh, but finally he reached his destination. In fact, it was extraordinary how well the railway system coped throughout the war. Arrivals may often have been late, but those great workhorses the steam locomotives pounded away in all weathers and even during air raids, providing a life-line where fuel restrictions made road transport available to the forces only.

On the day before the wedding, a blizzard blew up and continued for hours. The snow piled higher and higher on roads and pavements until even the trams had to give up, but trains still got through, and soon my parents-in-law-to-be arrived with Wullie's parents from Glasgow. Anxiously, we waited for the bridegroom, who eventually arrived with his sister-in-law Gladys from Norfolk, where she and his brother Jim lived. On his way to Scotland he had visited Gladys and her little boy Billy, who, with Jim also in the army, were on their own. A quick arrangement for Gladys' mother to look after Billy, and off they went. Unfortunately, they were minus the best man, Wullie. The army had decided not to give both of the lads leave at the same time, which came as a great disappointment, particularly to Mr and Mrs Young who had been so looking forward to seeing Wull again. However, it was of no use complaining.

The wedding Saturday dawned clear and cold. The storm had hardly abated during the night, and to get into the taxi I had to step down from

76

the piled-up snow on the pavement. Arriving at the church, Ruthrieston South on Holburn Street, where our family were members, we found that the minister, the Rev James Youngson, had been caught in a snowdrift on his way back from a funeral, and so the congregation had to wait in the cold, unheated church for half an hour. Most of the congregation, that is – Grandpa Masson refused to budge from the nice warm taxi! Grandma too kept warm in her black fur coat with large collar, which, as she said later, she was 'affa gled o".

Bill had joined the army as a rookie, but by this time he was very much the military man. When asked, 'Do you take this woman to be your wedded wife?' he quite forgot himself and replied smartly, 'I do, sir'. A ripple of laughter ran round the congregation; I managed to keep a straight face, as did the minister (just), but if Bill had saluted as well I would positively have dropped!

At home after the ceremony, our good neigbours had set out hired tables with Granny's damasks, wine glasses, wedding cake, flowers, telegrams, etc. What a welcome sight it was. The night before, my mother, with help from the other women, had prepared the Scotch Broth, steak, vegetables, potatoes, etc, and big bowls of the Scotch trifle at which she excelled. Due to shortage of sugar, the two-tier wedding cake from Mitchell and Muil's had no icing, but it had a nice frilled paper decoration around each of the tiers, and it looked lovely.

It was a very happy reception, and our neighbours, Mrs Wilson and Mrs Ross, served the meal and joined us in the toasts – sherry for the ladies and whisky for the men. Our last-minute elected best man, my uncle Andrew Masson, spoke of the times when he took me to the Starrie as a child, remarking what a 'pest o' a quinie' I had been to him. He also read out the telegrams, one of which I still have. Sent by Wullie Young's sister Peggy, it read: 'Go to it with all your might – No coupons required for tonight!' Topical indeed ....

Later, at the ensuing party, a girl named Dolly with whom I worked sang us 'Apple Blossom Time', which, recorded by the Andrews Sisters, was a big favourite on the American Forces Network throughout much of the war. Wedding photos had been taken earlier at a studio with Bill in Army uniform, my sister Margaret on her blue bridesmaid's dress and Andrew in civvies. We smiled for the camera on that cold, snowy January day, which was perhaps brightened a little by the bouquet of daffodils (my favourite flower) that I carried.

Bill and I left the reception at 10.30 p.m. in a taxi which, bombarded with snowballs, slithered and slid its way along Riverside Drive and up Victoria Road to my Aunt Daisy's house, where we were to spend the next two nights. A warm fire greeted us, and a small table was set out with tea and biscuits. Daisy certainly did her best to make us comfortable on that cold winter's night.

We spent a short honeymoon at Bill's home amid even deeper snow. For my going-away outfit (by 'going away' I mean a Pullman journey to Glasgow with half of the wedding party!) I wore one of the first Utility coats. It had no buttons or trimmings, and only a tie-belt, but it was warm and cosy, and was a lovely shade of blue. I felt very much a bride in it. Burgundy-coloured woollen dress with matching suede handbag and shoes completed my attire.

Towards the end of Bill's leave, we had to return to Aberdeen, and Gladys had to come with us on her way back to England. We left late at night on a darkened train, lucky to find an empty compartment in which we could stretch out on the seats. I had just wound a pink bed-jacket around my feet when the someone opened the door and from the eery blue light of the corridor came a voice which said 'Oh sorry – I hope I haven't woken the baby'. Gladys never felt such a 'gooseberry' in her life, and we still laugh about that journey with three of us on the honeymoon train!

Just like so many other couples in that time of war, we had to part, and it would be four months before we would meet again for another week of Bill's leave. After Bill and Gladys had left on the train that Sunday night, we sat and listened to Winston Churchill on the wireless, urging the nation to think only of victory over the 'Nazzies'. A morale-boosting speech as always, followed by the familiar voice of Vera Lynne. 'We'll Meet Again', 'When the Lights Come On Again' – I felt so sad.

Sitting around the fire, our topic of conversation was of course the wedding. I was very proud of the way in which everything had been done, with the well-set tables, the delicious meal and the party afterwards. 'But where', I asked, 'did everybody sleep?' 'Oh, we managed fine', my mother replied, 'Except that a cousin complained that she was cold and I told her to use her fur coat as an extra blanket'. 'Nae pleasin' some folk!', she added. Actually, some were given beds at the Wilsons' and the Rosses', which was typical of their generosity.

On the following Monday morning I was back behind my counter at Woolworth's, wondering how I might be able to get away for Bill's next leave. Having used up my annual holidays, it would be impossible, I knew, and from then on I did not feel so enthusiastic about working for Woolie's. Some weeks later, on a day when the manager was in even more of a fault-finding mood than usual, I went during my lunch hour to the 'Broo' in Market Street and volunteered for munitions work. Before long, Woolie's was in the past and I was busy on a six-week training course, held in a building by Peacock's Close in the Castlegate. This soon proved to be the most enjoyable time of my working life. The trainees were all young married girls; I was 19 (Bill, incidentally, was 22) and we all had husbands in the Forces. We all looked forward to our wages of 39 shillings (nearly £2!)

per week, which augmented the meagre service pay of 30 bob.

Our instructors were a pleasant middle-aged man and a lady with grey-ing hair. They were very tolerant of our high spirits and of the mistakes that we made in the early stages. Each of us was given a vice, a piece of metal and a hacksaw, and was instructed to draw in chalk an exact square on the metal. We then had to cut round the square with the saw. This was not very easy, but gradually we became more adept, even managing one day to turn out a spanner! We had a canteen for tea breaks, and in it we had much hilarious conversation over tea and buns. We all had so much in common, and I made a special friend – a girl named Evelyn Laing, who had previously worked in a shoe shop. I had at first found her a little stand-offish, but we soon struck up a friendship which lasted for quite some time. Evelyn was a slightly-built girl with a bright, open face. She wore discreet make-up, and her hair was obviously carefully curled each morning before work. I never seemed to have time for that before my morning dash for the tram – a touch of lipstick was all that I managed!

Through tea-time gossip and girl-talk, we gained little cameos of each other's lives. Some laughter was essential in those grim times, with terri-ble tales filtering in of the treatment handed out to surrendering Allied troops by the Japanese after the fall of Singapore that February. There was great bitterness at the mismanagement of the defence of Singapore by the 'top brass', and its loss, coming after those of Hong Kong and Manila in January, spawned a feeling of futility at home. Meanwhile, as the news sank in, thousands of men were being marched off to Changi Jail.

By May 1942 the British 14th Army under General Wingate was in retreat from the Japanese in Burma, its brave men beaten back in the bit-ter fight amidst the rotting, stinking jungle, plagued by leeches and chok-ing humidity. Struggling through torrential rain and mud, and racked with diseases, the remnants finally reached haven in India. But the 'Chindits' would be back.

Our neighbours, the Rosses, were devastated when news came that Margaret's husband Johnny had been taken prisoner of war by the Japa-nese. This was the last that they heard of him until four years later when the Red Cross informed Margaret of his death in a prisoner of war camp. Many thousands of other families were shaken by similar news.

All too soon, our six weeks of training for munition work ended. We were now considered to be fully-fledged machinists or (as in my case) fitters. I was sorry to lose my friends' company, especially that of Evelyn and a tall blonde girl named Jean, who later drove a tram in the city. To-gether, we went to sign on at the 'Broo' in order to be allocated work. To my dismay, I was offered a job somewhere near Luton, which I most em-phatically declined. In so doing, I lost my entitlement to financial support from the Labour Exchange, but soon, to my relief, I received instructions to report to Aberdeen Motors in Union Row.

Just before this, Bill and I had a stroke of luck. He was given seven precious days' leave, and I was able to travel south and stay with him at his home. As usual, we broke our journey to visit Wullie's parents at Cambuslang. They were especially anxious to have news of their son, knowing as we did that soon the boys would be away to fight.

These were worrying times indeed, but yet there was always some episode or other to provide laughter. Making one's way through blacked-out streets on a moonless night was not the easiest of exercises, as those who have tried it will know. Apart from the risk of accident, it was all too easy to lose one's bearings and become lost, even when close to home. I found that out one honeymoon leave when we stayed overnight with the Youngs. Bill and I decided to go and see 'Yankee Doodle Dandy', starring James Cagney, at the small cinema in the town's main street. It was only five minutes away from the house, and off we went, happy to be on our own for a while, enjoying the film from the seclusion of the back row seats. At the end of the show, we drifted out with the crowd into the pitch darkness, when suddenly I realised that I had become separated from Bill. I was completely disorientated, and quite frightened. My feet found the edge of the pavement, but I didn't attempt to cross the road; too many people had been killed or injured in the busier streets where darkened vehicles passed like ghosts in the night. Suddenly, the light of a pocket torch shone on my face and Bill's voice asked 'Where on earth did you get to? One minute you were there and the next you had disappeared!' I didn't like to tell him that I had followed the wrong khaki-clad figure out of the cinema!

At home in Kaimhill, our blackout curtains were drawn (usually by my young brother John) over the windows well before the decreed time. At Bill's home in the country, which was more isolated and where ARP wardens were less in evidence, things were a little more casual, but still no-one put a light on before first drawing the curtains. One night I went into a bedroom and, crossing the floor in the dark, found that the window was open. A night breeze blew in and something furry came straight towards me, rolling across the floor as I tried to close the window. Nervous of country life at the best of times, I flew back to the living room, convinced that some animal had jumped in through the open window. The family ran to the bedroom, pulled the blackout curtain and switched on the light to find on the floor a large furry hat which had been blown off the the window sill by the strong breeze. That moment confirmed that country life was not for me!

Returning to my new employment in munitions, on my first tram journey to Union Row from Bridge of Dee on that May morning in 1942, I felt just a little trepidation about commencing work in this strange environment. Arriving at Aberdeen Motors in my working garb of navy blue dungarees, I found that the workplace was just a large room with a high glazed roof which let in plenty of light. It was very much male dominated, with a few women working at machines on one side while men stood at similar machines on the other.

The pleasant-mannered foreman allocated me a bench at which, with a micrometer, I measured steel components from the machines, putting to one side any that did not come up to standard. Although I had trained to be a fitter, a man in oily dungarees tending one of the machines was the fitter, and he was not slow to make that clear. 'Served my time – took five years', he said, grinning, 'How long did you serve?' When I told him 'Six weeks', his grin became a derisive laugh which I did not appreciate. Women trained for munitions worked hard, their fingers skilfully guiding machines through the intricacies of turning out thousands of metal parts for the war effort. The survival of Britain depended on it, and I found nothing funny about that.

Furthermore, women received approximately half the wage of men. When we discovered that we were frequently working until 10 o'clock at night for only £2 10s (£2.50) a week while the men were receiving £4 10s, there was a visit en masse to the manager's office. 'Not fair', we lamented; 'Government orders', he replied brusquely,

'Nothing to do with me!' And that was that. I sat with the girls at lunch break, missing the lively chatter of the training centre as we conversed among ourselves about our husbands and their leave, etc, while the men sat smoking, no doubt resenting this female invasion of what used to be their exclusive domain. However, we simply had to accept our lot, as Aberdeen had nothing like the scope in munitions work that cities further south, with their giant factories, could offer. But on the other hand, Aberdeen did not have the daily and nightly air raids that those factories attracted.

Life at home was rather dull without our soldier lads. I wrote a letter every second evening, and of course received plenty from Bill. Under the flap of the envelope, I would write 'S.W.A.L.K.' (Sealed With a Loving Kiss). The war news was not good, with our Desert rats in North Africa being beaten back by Rommel's army. Rationing and austerity ruled our lives; bread was a strange grey colour, and when father brought home a beautiful white loaf that he had baked in his ship, we treasured every slice. Not a crumb was wasted. My sister made excellent jam tarts using the rather lard-like National Margarine. A little surplus of sugar and we made toffee which my younger brothers and sisters enjoyed while busy with their nightly homework under the strict supervision of my mother. So many schools were occupied by the military that part-time teaching had to be introduced in some of those that were still functioning, and later in the war married lady teachers, who would previously have been barred, were brought back to to do this. My mother was good with homework problems, especially mathematical ones. I felt some sympathy towards the younger members of our family when, unable to understand the solution when it was found, they were given a dunt on the shoulder and called 'a feel gype'!

I had my own kind of problems, the main one (shared by all working girls with husbands in the forces) still being how to obtain time off when Bill came home on leave. He was due to arrive on embarkation leave that June, and then he would be off to war, probably in the Middle East or India. He would be coming straight to Aberdeen after a quick visit to his parents in Lanarkshire. When working, especially on a 10 o'clock night, I would have so little time to be with him that I decided on a desperate measure – I would simply beg our genial foreman for time off. I could have pretended to be ill, but I didn't like that, so, almost in tears, I went and pled my case. At first he replied flatly, 'No, not possible', but finally I persuaded him to let me have the time in lieu of holiday. We spent the leave time quietly, if 'quiet' is the correct word to describe life among our two crowded households. A visit to the pictures provided a welcome relief from it all. Wullie came to Aberdeen to see our family, which had given him a home from home for so long, then too soon the leave was over and it was time for tearful farewells. Railway stations were always packed with what seemed to be hundreds of people as uniformed personnel boarded trains. Kitbags with name and number were hoisted aboard, then the whistle blew and wives, sweethearts and relatives surged forward to wave until the train was out of sight.

Bill had been promoted to Sergeant before his last leave, and we were all very proud of him. His unit had been transferred from the Gordon Highlanders to the Royal Artillery after anti-tank training; there would be empty months before his first airmail letter with an address would reach me, and under wartime security no destinations were divulged, so I could only surmise as to where he might be bound. Later, we found out that the Regiment had travelled back North and had boarded a troopship which in July 1942 lay off Tail Of the Bank, on the Clyde. We read our daily papers, listened to radio news bulletins, and watched the Pathé and Movietone newsreels at the pictures, but the media seemed to bring no good news, only sadness at the mounting toll of losses at sea. In August 1942 George, Duke of Kent, was killed in a plane crash – war knew no boundaries of position or creed.

My work at munitions turned out to be short-lived. As the weeks went on, I became increasingly nauseated each morning by the oily smell of the machinery, and, feeling thoroughly sick, would rush out to stand over one of our ARP fire buckets, which were required to be kept in strategic positions in all buildings, although the use to which I put them did not appear in any Government statute or directive! The men in the workplace were older and married, and quickly recognised the signs and symptoms of pregnacy. I put up with their jokes and innuendos with the required good humour. The girls were much more sympathetic, especially one young woman who was still working though in her fifth month, but then, as she said, she had suffered no sickness at all, and was very much in need of the salary. With Bill's promotion to Sergeant, I was slightly better off, as my army pay book now entitled me to collect just under £3 each week at the Post Office.

When my parents saw the situation, they made their displeasure very clear. The family was already a large one, with my younger sister not yet a year old and my husband off to God-knew-where, with the risk of never returning. This additional worry was the last thing that they needed, and by the time that my mother had finished pointing out that much I was wishing that I had joined the ATS, WAAF or WRENS instead of getting married!

Already our neighbours the Wilsons had two grandchildren, the children of their daughter Chrissie, whose husband was in the RAF. The Ross family had two children in the household, as had the Reids – it was a case of 'house full' for most, and would remain so for years until the housing situation improved. However, my mother never worried about anything for long. She seemed to have an inbuilt ability to accept philosophically life's ups and downs, and I fully appreciated and accepted her words when she explained that her strong reaction was purely out of concern for my welfare in the times in which we lived, although at the same time I did inwardly wonder why, in that case, we had such a large family when my father's job at sea was so dangerous! So many war-time weddings, so many babies being born, and so many men being shipped abroad, wishing to leave behind some tangible evidence of their existence on this earth; the maternity hospitals were full to capacity.

After a wait of many weeks, I at last received an air-mail letter from Bill, giving his posting address. As my father had surmised, he was in Egypt, at a place near Cairo. We later found out that the place was called El Alamein. As the Suez Canal was held by the Axis powers, his troop ship had taken the long route round Africa to Capetown and then up the coast to Egypt, hence the lengthy silence. At least this perilous journey through U-Boat infested waters was over, but ahead lay even more danger in the hard-fought desert battles that were to come.

With secrecy paramount, road signs, railway station name-boards, place names on vans and lorries, and even ships' names on sailors hats had disappeared, the hat bands now simply stating 'HMS ——'. Mail to and from the war zone was scrutinised, and it was most embarrassing to see the word 'Censored' stamped on very personal letters. Anything considered untoward would be scored through with blue pencil, so letters were apt to be just a little stilted at first, though we soon got used to it and stopped caring. On one air-mail letter to me, Bill ended the address with 'Bonnie Scotland'. The censor scored through the word 'Bonnie'. Wullie Young's mother Maggie ended all her letters to him with 'Roll On the Big Ship', but no-one seemed to take any notice of that!

My short period of employment in munitions at an end, I was back at home again helping with the household chores, rather to my mother's relief. I received no sickness benefit that I can remember, and no 'broo', as I had left voluntarily, so the army pay was my only income. 'We'll manage fine', my mother said. We had only my sister Margaret's wage to augment that brought home by father, but then no-one that we knew had much money either, and things were still better than they had been during the Depression. We were all better fed, and women could take over jobs when men were called up to the forces.

Radio programmes like 'Music While You Work' helped to keep Britain's factories humming, and 'Workers' Playtime' was often broadcast from the huge munitions works in England. As I have already mentioned, these and the large cities in which they were situated made priority targets for German bombers, while in Scotland the important shipbuilding centre of Clydebank was blitzed and entire families were wiped out in its crowded tenements. Aberdeen's sirens sounded often, especially during daylight, but the daily round went on. Having got over the intial discomforts of my condition, I could go out to the pictures again, or take the time-honoured walk around the Friday Castlegate market, which still held immense fascination for the Aberdonian. Goods could be found there that were now scarce, and pre-war china was much sought after. After this walk around, my mother and I would go for tea and scones at John E Esslemont's in King Street, or if we were in George Street we would go to The Buttery. One day while we were walking along Broad Street the sirens sounded, and we could see some activity in the sky above us, so we quickly took refuge in a concrete air-raid shelter opposite Marischal College until the all-clear. I remember buying a coat that day, using some of my own coupons and some of the family's. This 'swagger coat', as it was termed (utility, of course), was in a nice shade of blue, and it served well as a maternity garment.

All the while, the sight of the postie each day was a welcome one, bringing me Bill's letters from the other side of the world. There were photos from Cairo, where Bill had been on leave with some of the other men from the 126 Anti-Tank Regiment MEF (Middle East Force). They showed the men in their usual garb for such a hot country - shorts and shirts of lightweight material (khaki-coloured, of course) and forage caps.

I think these garments were referred to in the Army's abbreviated jargon as K.D.'s, standing presumably for 'Khaki Drill'. Shoulder flashes and stripes were worn on the shirts, Bill, as a Sergeant, having three stripes.

Soon it was time for me to attend the ante-natal clinic beside Cockie Hunter's (formerly the Sick Children's Hospital) in Castle Terrace, off the Castlegate. This very small building, which had been the city's maternity hospital before the completion of the present Royal Infirmary at Foresterhill in the early 1930s, was always crowded, and there was always a long wait to be seen by one of the harrassed doctors, many of whom were actually students. However, we girls passed the time with a good gossip, and I spoke to many whose husbands were also serving in the Forces abroad.

Nowadays, a wide variety of maternity clothes is available for young mothers-to-be, but that was not the case during the war. We would sew tape on to our skirts and tie it at the appropriate point to accommodate our figures as they increased, a cotton smock concealing all evidence of this make-do, as it was the done thing for women to camouflage their condition. Where nowadays television shows the world the process of childbirth at all its stages, we were told nothing at all about it. Everything was in fact very low-key, although correct diet was strongly emphasised. 'Drink plenty of milk, and take orange juice and the iron tablets provided for a few pence.' I seem to remember that cards were given out for presenting to the milkman to claim a free pint in those rationed times. During the late summer months I walked a lot with my mother, who wheeled baby Wilma in her pram. With all the fresh air and exercise I looked and felt very fit indeed, and I sent snaps out to Bill.

In this war, Britain had never so far had a major victory, however much the mass rescue at Dunkirk might have been hailed as one. Efforts to free Norway had proved futile. The summer of 1942 passed; then suddenly at 9.40 p.m. on 23 October a thousand British heavy guns opened fire, splitting the still desert air as, with a thunderous bombardment, the Battle of El Alamein began. The aim was to push the Germans out of North Africa, and five days of fierce and bloody conflict ensued before the German defences were finally broken, with heavy casualties on both sides. The battle went on for many months, involving thousands of Indian, Commonwealth and British troops. The Americans were there too, facing the Vichy French as sea landings were made in Tunisia. Again there were heavy casualties on what was then French soil. At last, on 12th-13th May 1943 the end of the hard-fought desert war was proclaimed, and in honour of this the first Allied victory Winston Churchill decreed that 'All church bells will be rung'. And so they were. At home, we knew all the place names that had been mentioned in the news as we avidly followed the progress of our troops up to their victory at Tunis. The so-familiar voice of Winston Churchill proclaimed, 'This is not the end. It is not even the beginning of the end, but it is the end of the beginning.' Before El Alamein we never had a victory: after it we never had a defeat.

During the months of battle I received many letters from Bill, headed 'a hole in the desert'. No place names were allowed, but I knew the danger that he was in, and I prayed every night for his safe return, as well as that of Wullie and the other lads in his unit who we had got to know through their visits to us. I learned much later that just before one of the fiercest battles of the campaign, the battle of the Mareth Line on 20-21 March, Bill received our cablegram telling him of the birth of his daughter. He told us later that he had a bottle of whisky in his kitbag, and each man on the anti-tank gun toasted our health and congratulated their sergeant, the happy father!. The Germans threw all hell at them, and with Stukas screaming overhead and shells bursting all around them, he prayed to survive to see his baby.

The baby's arrival, at Foresterhill Maternity Hospital that March, came as a short, sharp and very painful experience for me. I had travelled to the hospital in a taxi with my mother, she and my sister Margaret having summoned the cab from the phone box near the shop at Kaimhill. I entered the hospital at 6.30 a.m. and my baby was born at 8.15 a.m. As I am wont to relate to my family even now, no drugs were given, not even an aspirin. I felt quite alone in an alien world peopled by strangers with faces covered by green masks, some looking sympathetically at me, others with brisk authority. I didn't know who was making all the noise, but apparently it was me, as I was given the blessed relief of a mask of gas and air. A voice asked me where my husband was (not that husbands were allowed to be present at births as they are now), and I replied 'North Africa'. Soon after, in silence, I became the mother of a fine healthy girl. My mother and our neighbour, Mrs Stewart, came to visit me that evening. The first thing that I said to my mother, rather accusingly, was 'You said it would be jist like toothache – some toothache!' I then told her that the baby was to be her namesake, Elizabeth Masson Kilgour, and she shed a little tear about that.

Confined to bed for seven days, as was then the rule, I made friends with the girl in the next bed. She was of about my own age, and her husband was, like mine, in North Africa. In a bed at the end of the ward was a youngish-looking woman with blonde hair. She, we were told, had had no less than fourteen pregnancies and seventeen children. My companion and I looked on this phenomenon with great awe. That night her husband came to visit her, in civilian clothes and bearing a large bunch of flowers. We felt very envious, not having our husbands to visit us, but I piped up, 'If he was my husband I'd take a gun and shoot him!' We had come to the conclusion that we were having no more children!

The words 'feeding-bottle' were apparently bad ones that that time, as all mothers in the hospital had to breast-feed their babies. One young girl wept to her mother on every visit that she was being forced to do this, and was having a difficult time. On the day that she went home, her grim-faced mother wrapped the baby up tightly in his shawl and exited with the words, 'C'mon hame an' ye'll get a bottle o' Copie milk!'

One night during my stay in hospital the air raid sirens went. Nurses hurried around carrying the babies to the bottom floor of the building where I presumed there was some sort of shelter. We mothers were left on the upper floor to face whatever danger the night might bring, as the nurses could never have coped with sheltering all the patients. The AA guns opened up, but after a noisy half hour the all-clear sounded and we breathed great sighs of relief. This incident may appear trivial, but it was an eerie and quite frightening experience.

My mother-in-law and Mrs Young travelled up by train to see the new baby. Wullie's mother had knitted some lovely baby clothes and bootees, and Bill's mother had also been busy with the needles, knitting jackets in the small amount of spare time that she had at the farm. My 15 month-old sister Wilma was not at all welcoming towards this new arrival that took up so much of my attention, but I made a point of sitting her on my knee and making a fuss of her. My other two little sisters, Eleanor and Nora, were very excited, especially when told that they were now both aunties! Nora was five years old and Eleanor seven. James, the eldest of my three brothers (the other two, John and Andrew, were still at school), had become an apprentice with a firm of plumbers in the city, while my eldest sister Margaret, now seventeen, was working in the 'glove factory' – Messrs Kilgour Walker's in Chapel Street. Later she became an office worker. Ours was therefore a large and busy household.

Grandma Masson, now a very proud Great-Grandma, came to see the baby, taking her from the beautiful pre-war pram that I had managed to purchase for her, and 'walking' her about, calling her 'my golden girl'. This spritely, youthful-looking lady had (as she put it) 'got herself something to do' – cleaning work at a Mitchell and Muil's bakery at the going rate of 1s. 6d. an hour. Never the sort to sit around, she revelled in taking on work again.

She continued to bring us all the news from Fittie. 'The Fittie folk', she told us, 'are not allowed up the pier – the sodgers guard it!' The Torry Battery, across the channel between the North and South piers, was similarly out of bounds – 'Full o' sodgers an' guns'. High on the cliff top, the army had a panoramic view of the bay, and anti-aircraft guns were always kept at the ready to fire on enemy aircraft as they flew in over the sea. I am told that the army personnel at Fittie were well looked after by the local folk, and sometimes there were little impromptu dances on the pier, with an accordionist providing the music. So people sought to make the most of every day in the midst of the war.

That important Middle East victory of Lt General Bernard Montgomery's 8th Army had given us something to celebrate at last. Next, the 'Desert Rats', as the 7th Armoured Division was known, moved on with the others to the next stage in the conflict. Bill's unit had served in the campaign with the 4th Indian Division, and our own Highland regiments had also been in the forefront of the fighting. It had in fact, I learned, been Bill's battery that had fired the signal shot for the battle to commence on that fateful night at El Alamein.

Comforts out there were few. A fag and a brew-up of tea in an old petrol can had to do when not even a tin of 'McConnachie's', the now-famous food manufactured in Fraserburgh for the Armed Forces, could be provided. On one occasion, not even proper cigarettes came up the line to the eagerly waiting men. Instead they received an offering called 'Victory V's', which were declared vile. 'Must be made from camel dung', the men said, but they had nothing else. Like Pashas, India was blamed for their origin.

One cold March day I went along to the Registrar's Office in Union Terrace to register my daughter's birth. I must have looked poorly (I certainly felt so, not having quite recovered from the birth), as after taking the marriage certificate and asking all the necessary questions, the tall middle-aged man behind the counter lifted the wooden flap and allowed me to sit on a chair by the bright coal fire that burned in the grate behind him as he completed the birth certificate for me in beautiful italic writing. This incident has always remained in my mind, and I recall that I felt noticeably better afterwards.

Soon after, I received a 'chitty' enabling me to collect my maternity money – £2 and 5 shillings graciously granted to us by our Government! On the morning of my departure from the hospital, I and a couple of other young mothers had to go to Matron's office to arrange payment for our stay, as there was no free treatment in those days. Matron asked me what my income was and where it came from. Eventually she inquired, 'Would you manage to pay five shillings?' I agreed to this, and so discharged my debt to my country's medical services.

Sometimes Bill's letters would arrive in small batches, due no doubt to the long distances involved, but it was truly wonderful to sit down and read them. I sent photos, of course, and long letters describing everything from our daughter's birth to her weight and progress. We were among the lucky ones; our good neighbour Mrs Ross's daughter heard nothing at all of her husband. Not even the Red Cross could get anywhere with the Japanese, and there were many thousands of similar cases. The generation that had suffered so much during the 'hungry thirties' was now having to cope with even more tragedy, which it did with great stoicism.

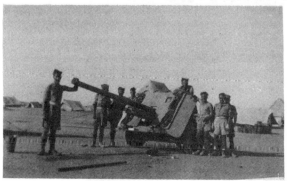

Top: Bill in desert uniform
Bill (front centre) and "his lot" at Cairo, 1942
Bottom: The 17-pounder anti-tank gun, Egypt 1942

Top right: Bill and Wull, Cairo 1942
Centre: Army mates, Cairo 1942
Bottom: Friends who came through so much together –
Bill (right) and Wull, Alexandria, 1942

CHAPTER 7

If absence made the heart grow fonder for Bill and I, there were lots of people for whom it did not. Long separations due to war service could end in a letter which even in those days was known as a 'Dear John', telling of infidelity, and many a marriage or engagement was terminated in this way. The cruelty of such a blow to a man serving in a theatre of war can only be imagined, but temptation was everywhere for young women and girls in a country crowded with servicemen, even though it would be naive to expect men on leave abroad to be entirely without blemish.

Often I would wonder what had become of all the boys I had known in peacetime when I went dancing with my chums, walked the mat on a Sunday, or bought a cheap seat at the pictures. In particular I remembered the warm summer of 1939, meeting up with Madge Grant, the two other girls and the quartet of boys at 'The Queen' before walking perhaps to Hazlehead Park, talking and laughing all the way there and back. No money to spend, but happy with Bill Masson from the West end, Davie Paton from Hilton, and their two friends.

Just two weeks before the birth of my daughter, I went with my sister to the Odeon cinema to see the film 'Mrs Miniver', starring Greer Garson. It was a 'weepie', so to revive our spirits we went for a fish tea at the old Regal Cafe on the other side of Justice Mill Lane. We had just sat down when I noticed some soldiers. One was in hospital blues, denoting wounded; it was Bill Masson, and we smiled as we recognised each other, but in my condition I didn't want to draw attention to myself so we didn't speak. When the soldiers got up to leave, I saw to my grief that Bill was walking on crutches – he had lost a leg. I believe he was wounded in North Africa, and it came to me as a revelation of the harsh realities of war.

On special occasions such as our wedding anniversary or my birthday, my husband would send a cablegram home. Only such stilted phrases as 'Wish I could be with you at this time' were allowed, but I treasured every one. On 21 April 1943 it was Bill's 24th birthday, and my thoughts were with him more than ever. I wondered where he was and what new dangers he might be having to face, little knowing that that very night we at home would be facing great dangers of our own in the heaviest of all bombing raids on Aberdeen.

As the North African campaign raged in Tunisia, Germany's cities suffered very heavy daylight raids by the combined forces of Bomber Command and the American Air Force with its Flying Fortresses – giant bombers with ten-man crews. In retaliation, Hitler ordered the Luftwaffe in occupied Norway to bomb areas within easy reach, Aberdeen being one of these. Unusually for the time, all of our family was at home that evening with the exception of my father who was out at sea on his trawler. Dusk had fallen, enough to make it necessary to draw the blackout curtains in case some sharp-eyed ARP warden should hand us a fine for showing as much as a chink of light. The glass doors at the front and back had to be covered, a chore detested by my two youngers brothers who were usually detailed to carry it out, and who by this time had become experts. My little daughter, just one month old, had been fed and put in her pram for the night, as I had yet to obtain a cot for her. The other two little ones were just about to go to bed upstairs when the wail of the sirens began like a banshee in the night. As the stomach-turning noise went on, we felt our usual apprehension; the sirens had barely stopped when all of a sudden it seemed that all hell had broken loose. Amid the terrifying sound of gunfire, I grabbed the baby from her pram. As the heavy German planes passed overhead the bombs began dropping; somehow most of us managed to cower under the Morrison shelter, which fortunately had been brought back into the living room, but as there was not room for everybody my mother and sister took refuge in the cupboard under the stairs. I remember urging the others to 'keep your legs in', and as I sat there clutching my baby, my little sister Wilma sitting unconcernedly playing with some clothes-pegs, I prayed 'Please God don't let us get a direct hit'. Each screaming whine and terrible explosion seemed to come closer, while gunfire and cannon shell raked the city.

In town, people leaving cinemas looked with terrified amazement as the massed heavy bombers of the Luftwaffe suddenly appeared out of the night sky, too low for the searchlights to fasten on to them. Twenty-nine Dornier 217's, each with a 2,200 kilogramme bomb-load, came in waves of ten, dropping flares over the city's North side. They flew so fast and low that the gunners at Torry Battery and the fighter defences were taken by surprise. Their first stick of bombs demolished a block at the Gordon Barracks, and thereafter their deadly cargo was spead far and wide, the North side suffering most as fires raged and people died under tons of rubble. This was Blitzkrieg all right. When at long last the sirens sounded the all clear and we were able to crawl from our shelter after the worst night of the war that I can remember, relief gave way to tears. Our neighbours, drawn together by the common danger, came in to see that everyone was all right. Dazed and shocked, we felt that bed and sleep would be unthinkable that night, but after using up a considerable proportion of our weekly tea and sugar ration we eventually felt ready for sleep, thankful for our deliverance, but wondering 'How many more of the same?'

There was no sleep for the brave ARP, the rescue workers, the Fire Brigade and the police, who toiled to bring out the living, the injured and the dead from under the ruins of bombed buildings, a grim task which they carried out with great fortitude amd dedication. Next day the newspapers showed in words and pictures the destruction wreaked on what was simply described as 'a North-East city'. Soon, saddest of all, lists appeared in the local press naming the dead and injured, among whom could be seen whole families. Among the first casualties were members of defence crews, cut down before they could train their guns on the raiders, or could take cover. At Trinity Cemetery, a row of gravestones stands as memorials to those men, some of whom died subsequently of wounds sustained in the raid. Several were only 18 years old.

Among the many civilian casualties, I was saddened to hear of one little family in particular. Their burial ceremony at Trinity Cemetary was attended by full military band and, as press photographs show, a large sympathetic crowd. Earlier, I related how, during the time when I worked in the bakery at Catherine Street, I would go to the little corner fish shop where I became friendly with the young assistant, who lived in the Bedford Road area. She and her three very young sons died when their house was bombed that night, and somewhere in one of the war zones a husband received the news that his wife and little ones had perished.

Press reports the day after the raid spoke of phosphorus bombs having caused the large fires in the city's northern quarter, and of indiscriminate bombing causing heavy damage over a wide area. Indeed, hardly any districts escaped entirely unscathed.

The next night, still feeling rather shaken despite the strange abililty that we had all developed to accept whatever fate held in store for us, our family was all in bed. I was reading an Agatha Christie novel while the baby slept peacefully in her pram next to me. All of a sudden the sirens wailed out their warning once again. I was in the front room on the ground floor, and I shouted to the others to come down to the Morrison Shelter. This they did, tumbling downstairs in their haste, with the exception of my mother, who once in bed hated to be disturbed. Hearing ominous sounds of gunfire, I frantically called her and she eventually appeared, fulminating about 'that bloody Hitler' and what she would do to him if she got her hands on him. Thankfully, this time the all-clear sounded after only an hour or so and we were able to troop back to our beds, myself to read another chapter of my book.

One fine Sunday morning in the spring of 1943, my mother and I walked with Elizabeth in her pram to Ruthrieston South Church for her baptism by the Rev Youngson, who had officiated at my wedding the previous year. Elizabeth was wrapped in a beautiful lacy white shawl knitted by the expert of them all, Mrs Blair of Neptune Terrace, whom I mentioned in my previous book and who was my Uncle Andrew's mother-in-law. A large congregation watched the baptism, and Mr Youngson's concluding words brought a lump to my throat, 'May God bless this child and her father who is a soldier, wherever he may be at this time'. Afterwards, members of the congregation commented on how good the baby had been, and asked where my husband was serving. I could only tell them that he was with the 8th Army somewhere in North Africa. We walked back home, where we had tea and a piece of the top tier of the wedding cake, which had kept excellently in its airtight tin. Such sheer luxury to be eating this rich fruity slice, served on a plate with the obligatory tiny portion of cheese. Of course, news of all this was duly sent to Bill, along with one or two snaps that I took with my Brownie box camera.

I was very worried when some time after this Bill's letters stopped. Every day I watched anxiously for the postman. The war had been going well for us, but heavy fighting was still going on in North Africa, and Tunis was not taken until May. When letters did come through again, they were from Beirut, Damascus and other places in Lebanon, 'Operation Lightfoot', as the entire 8th Army campaign was tagged, had taken the men out of Egypt, through Libya and on to Algeria, then finally to Tunis. Bill was safe, but 'his lot', as he called them, had been turned all the way back via Cairo to Palestine, where trouble had broken out. A photo of Bill taken in a street in Damascus showed him looking well and relaxed, dressed now in the usual Army uniform in place of the desert garb that he had worn for so long. No forage cap, either – instead he wore a beret, Army issue. I could only guess what sort of camp his regiment was in when Bill, much later, spoke of having escorted Jugoslavian refugees who were passing through. 'Poor, pathetic people', he said. Another photo that I received was of Bill and his eldest brother Jim, with whom he had met up in Derna during the advance – a small miracle among all these thousands of troops. 'Browned off' was a phrase that appeared frequently in his letters, and also 'Going to the pictures', after which he would name some of the films. He wrote of 'Going with Wull for a walk round the market', and I was glad to know that the two were still together. It seemed that after the long and bitter battles in the desert, boredom had set in, but I suppose that that might have been expected as a reaction after all that had gone before.

Rations continued to get smaller and our clothes shabbier. Wooden-soled shoes made their appearance and were worn by some, but on the whole were not very popular. Children's shoes wore out as quickly as ever, and running a home was becoming an ever-increasing burden. Doctors' fees were dreaded just as much as they had ever been during the Depression, although people who worked and paid for National Insurance stamps were provided for by being 'on the panel'. Just after leaving my employment I developed a quinsy throat, and the first thing our lady doctor asked me was whether I was 'on the panel'. As my stamps had not yet run out I was, and she was relieved to know that she could therefore visit me as often as was necessary without having to send me a hefty bill. Quinsy was a very painful ailment which could only be treated with M and B tablets. Penicillin was reserved for the armed forces at that time.

With the coming of another summer, our thoughts turned to picnics and to happy times in years gone by, picking the buckies from the warm shallow pools at the Bay of Nigg, playing on the beach, or swimming in the sea. We could of course still go to the beach, but whole stretches of it were disfigured by barbed wire and concrete tank-traps, reminders of the time not so long before when a Nazi invasion of Britain seemed imminent. We decided therefore on a picnic at the Duthie Park, and on the appointed day the entire family, including Granny and Grandpa from Fittie, set off along the banks of the Dee to our destination, Grandpa having (as always) been rather unwillingly dragged away from his boat-making and repairing. The fresh air, grass and flowers of the park were a treat, and even Spam sandwiches with National Margarine tasted good. Tea from a flask, milk (probably dried) for the children, and it was just like our al fresco spreads of times past. It was a joyous day, at the end of which we saw my grandparents on to their tram before heading home for an evening meal of skirlie and Spam (more of it!) with potatoes. Even though ration points were necessary just to get a tin of Spam, and cheese, tea and sugar were restricted to 2 ounces a week per ration card, no-one had to go without. Rations may have been meagre, but 'When it's done, it's done', as my mother said, digging up part of the garden to plant potatoes.

On one occasion, I travelled by train to Glasgow (6 shillings return on production of my army pay book) to visit Bill's folk. I sat in the compartment with the baby on my knee, the other passengers being a lady in a fur coat, her daughter (also well dressed) and a Naval man who I think was a Chief Petty Officer, an older fellow who had no doubt been in the thick of the terrible war at sea. They were nice friendly people, and made the time pass quickly. In his little case, of the kind that most Navy men carried, the CPO had a plentiful supply of cigarettes and a screw-top bottle of beer, which he passed to the two ladies. In a refined Glasgow accent, the two graciously accepted a cigarette and a drink from the bottle! On arriving at Buchanan Street Station, I was met by one of Bill's sisters and the others went their separate ways after wishing our sailor good luck and a safe voyage. Unlike on the trains from England, which were always jampacked, it had been a very easy journey. The war had broken down many social barriers and Britain was a far better place for that, even though a near-feudal system still persisted in some quarters. Many of the gentry who owned large country mansions and estates were forced to manage without large staffs. Moreover, with fuel rationing those large houses could no longer be heated as they had been before the war. With perhaps only a cook, a gardener and a scullery maid left, all either too old or (as many kitchen maids were) too young for call-up, it was a changed world, and it would never be the same again.

Owners of such estates and houses could of course still reap good harvests from their land, storing and preserving fruit and vegetables for their own use. Even the Royal Family reportedly curtailed extravagance by having their breakfast marmalade served in the jar instead of decanted into jam dishes, from which leftovers had previously been thrown out!

Another Christmas and Hogmanay passed, and as the New Year of 1944 dawned hope was in everyone's heart that this war might be ended before another long weary year had gone by. Glasses were raised to toast the success of our troops in Italy, facing a hard, bitter slog after taking Sicily. We had always pictured Italy as hot and sunny, but weather conditions in the battle zones were anything but that. British, Commonwealth and American troops were knee-deep in mud and water, in freezing temperatures which made progress almost impossible for the tired and battle-weary men.

Christmas Day in Scotland was still not celebrated with present-giving, exchanging of Christmas cards or Christmas dinner. Years were to pass before it was declared a holiday, and people in employment still worked as normal. In time of war, our Christian beliefs were felt deep within us. Hearing the age-old Christmas carols on the wireless brought to the surface feelings of great longing to see our loved ones, and the tears flowed easily. For the little ones, stockings were hung up at the fireplace in the traditional way for Santa to fill, and although 'Suntie' could not leave sweets, apples or oranges, a few little toys and other things still brought pleasure and excitement. I held my little daughter up to look at our framed wedding photograph, taken by Bon-Accord newspaper as we stood at the door of the church, and I said for her, 'Happy Christmas, Daddy'!

On Hogmanay nights my father, home from sea, liked to celebrate, so 1944 was brought in with the usual little party and with first-footing among our neighbours and a few members of the Forces who were present through family ties or friendships with the girls. The toast was always 'to absent friends'. I had a portable gramophone which I had seen advertised in the Evening Express and which I had bought for about £2 10s; the first record that I played on it was Bing Crosby singing 'White Christmas'. Glenn Miller and the superb American big bands were still all the rage, and we had quite a few of their records to dance to . Of course we also had Gladys Reid's favourite, 'Begin the Beguine'!

Since the end of the North Africa campaign, Bill's regiment seemed to be continually on the move, with letters arriving either several at a time or not at all. I had to send my letters to the usual cryptic Army postal addresses such as MEF, BDRA, etc, but as censorship had now been lifted somewhat, photos with place names on the back had become permissible. I never kept any of my husband's letters – they were so personal to me that having read them, I destroyed them. I did not at all fancy the idea of perhaps being bombed out of our house and having some stranger pick them up and read them. I was not the only one to think that way; some girls that I knew would tear up letters and fill a cushion with the paper pieces. Strange perhaps, and unsentimental maybe, but true.

My little daughter had her photograph taken so often that her progress could be easily seen by her father who had never met her. By this time she was able to walk, so one day I took her into town in the tram, and, held by reins, she toddled up George Street with me to Isaac Benzies, round which excellent store I always enjoyed a walk. This particular walk cost me 7s. 6d. when a certain determined little lady took hold of a wooden horse on wheels and would not let it go! It was just the right height for her, and pushing it by the handle she walked back with it towards Union Street. Spoiled by the family she may have been, but who could not have spoiled this golden-haired child with big brown eyes. Even at that age she was striking to look at, and I was so proud of her. I liked to buy nice clothes for her (subject to the usual rationing, of course), and to this end I decided to supplement my army pay of £3 5s. by taking on a cleaning job. An opportunity came my way when our life insurance lady told me that she had clients who required the services of a cleaner. I decided to give it a try, even though with the size of our family I had plenty to do at home, and so in due course I presented myself at a large and very classy flat in Broomhill Road. There I polished, Hoovered (only very posh people had Hoovers and vacuum cleaners!), dusted and cleaned for three hours, for which I received 4s. 6d. I also black-leaded the grate and the doorstep scraper. There was another cleaning lady, fairly elderly, who sat with an apron on her lap, cleaning brass flower planters and other objects. She chatted away to me as I worked, and we had a cup of tea together. 'An affa fine wifie', I told my mother. However, once I had earned enough to buy my little girl a coat and hat set I gave up the job, as things at home were hard enough to keep up with.

We always seemed to have somebody staying with us, and Wull's father and mother were regular and generous visitors. Wull's father, Geordie, was a miner, and as the coal pits now had staggered holidays we saw them quite often. Bill's father, who also had a background in the coal pits, returned to a mining job at this time. He was a winding engineer, responsible for the cages which, driven by a massive array of machinery, carried

Top left: With Elizabeth at 2 months, 1943
Top right: 1943
Bottom left: On the beach, 1943
Bottom right: Elizabeth at 15 months

the men up and down the pit shaft, from and to the coal face. Geordie Young actually worked at the coal face as a 'brusher' – a 'prop man' who kept the roof of coal overhead safe from collapse. Miners could buy seven tons of coal a year for just £1 per ton, and when Geordie put coal on our fire my mother would turn a shade of pale. She had to tell him how little coal we could get and how much it cost! At Bill's home they too had plenty of coal stored in the barn, and were able to make some money from eggs, pigs and poultry. We in Aberdeen were not in such a fortunate position, but tight as money was we enjoyed our evenings at the pictures and the bustle of city life, the shops and the Friday Castlegate market. Yes, Aberdeen was my town – no country life for me.

In the conditions of the time, it still remained a mystery to me how my mother managed to feed everyone, but she did, and all gratis. Mrs Young was a prolific knitter, and regularly presented the children with dresses, jumpers, socks and cardigans. The Youngs found our modern house very different from their little ground-floor but-an'-ben at Cambuslang, and very much enjoyed their visits. We were indeed lucky. Many people in the old houses, where outside toilets and washhouses were still the norm, continued to be without any facilities, and the war had stopped the building of new houses.

One popular film of this time was 'Desert Victory', an impressive account of what our men had just gone through in North Africa. We came away from a showing of it quite in awe. One thing that we noticed was that while the British and Commonwealth troops wore khaki drill shorts, desert boots, puttees and drill shirts, the Germans (and also the Americans when they first entered the war) sweltered in their regular long trousers! Throughout the war in the hot countries the British wore their shorts, reverting only to standard trousers when winter weather, as experienced in Italy, demanded it.

In preparation for the war's greatest battle, the coming assault on the fortress of Europe, thousands of Americans arrived in Britain to join with British and Allied troops in intensive training. Whole villages and other quiet backwaters in the South were cleared to house these men and their machines, and many more had to vacate their homes as flat land was taken over for aerodromes from which to launch the hundreds of bombers that would shortly hammer Berlin and other large cities in Germany. For some time, the American Airforce's B17 Flying Fortresses had been flying in daylight raids on Germany, but these proved too costly in men and machines, and now the Americans were flying out at night with Bomber Command.

Whichever side of the Mason-Dickson line the new arrivals hailed from, we in Britain called them 'Yanks'. They arrived in droves like some invading force, with cracks like 'We'll finish your war for you'. Fresh young fellows who had never seen combat, they now saw the devastation caused by the German bombing of our cities, and the war-weary people, shabby and living on severely rationed food while in their PX's and clubs they had all the provisions that they could hope for, sent by the American government for 'the boys over there'. In their own country and by their own choice they were known as GI's after the 'Government Issue' imprint on their clothing and other kit. I found out from a historian's talk on Grandholm Mills that the excellent quality of Hank, Buzz, Abe and Herb's uniforms was attributable to the fact that the material came from Grandholm, right here in Aberdeen!

Intensive training for battle in Europe was in progress by early 1944, and London was full of uniformed personnel on leave, particularly GI's. 'Live it up now – we may die later' was the sentiment, and live it up they did, thronging Piccadilly 'chasing the chicks' and looking for excitement. They had a baptism of fire when long-suffering, brave London became a target for Hitler once again, this time with his secret weapons, the V1 and then the V2 rocket. Known as 'doodle bugs' or 'buzz bombs', over a hundred of these, the first-ever long-range ballistic missiles, were launched from secret bases on the Continent. Crammed with explosive, they were powered by simple jet engines which stopped in time for them to fall to ground indiscriminately over a very wide area around their target. The horrific scenes that followed made the ominous sound of the approach of one of these rockets, followed by the even more ominous silence when the engine cut out, a new terror for London and the South of England.

Just after my little daughter took her first steps, I celebrated my 22nd birthday. Soon after, a parcel arrived from Bill. It contained six pairs of pure silk stockings (beautiful, with dark seams and contoured heels) and a silk dressing-gown for me, and little dresses for Elizabeth and Wilma. This was a luxurious present indeed, and I kept the stockings in an airtight screw-top jar. With the parcel came an ALC (Air Letter Card) bearing a CMF (Central Mediterranean Force) address – Bill was in Italy!

One day, two young soldiers arrived at our door, one, Jim, a brother-in-law of Wullie Young, and the other a lad named Davie, who hailed from the Borders. Just eighteen, they were among the younger conscripts which the war effort was calling up for the D-Day force, D-Day being now on everybody's mind. Older men were also being conscripted for intensive training, although it was anybody's guess when the important day would come. The two pals were made welcome and given a meal. 'Home from home', they said in appreciation. Soon they were off to England to join with the force of two million who, with all the equipment of war, were waiting to cross the Channel.

Life at home, meanwhile, was hard work, but was relieved now and then by an outing to a dance, which gave an opportunity to dress up a little and do what I had always loved doing. These dances usually took the form of little 'hops' in aid of the Red Cross or some other of the relief groups in the war effort. My Aunt Daisy, who loved to dance, asked me to go to one with her. Her husband Andy had never learned the art himself but didn't mind when she went for an evening out, and we had an enjoyable time, with tea and a sandwich during the interval. My mother's 'Copie Guildie' held dances too, so off I went with her to Mitchell and Muil's Rooms (so many venues then) where we did Quadrilles, d'Alberts and other dances which I had learned at Old Time nights at the City Ballroom in George Street earlier in the war. These were remarkably popular with younger folk as well as with the older generation. The figures were quite intricate, and there would be frowns of annoyance if a wrong move was made in the sequences, but the music was good and the evening most exhilarating.

Couples could often be heard singing the war-time tunes as they danced. One number that was particularly popular for the last dance was 'Goodnight Sweetheart', a very sentimental song which always brought a lump to my throat as I thought of my husband who had been so far away for so long.

So there we were in the early part of 1944, huddling around our small coal fire in the depths of a snowy winter, eating wheat flakes for breakfast (no corn flakes having been seen since the start of the war), spreading our bread with the oily National Margarine, eating National Dried Egg and Spam, mixing up National Dried Milk when the fresh milk ran out, and looking forward to the occasional little off-ration luxury that 'Griggie's', continued to slip us in return for our registering some of our ration books.

We read the papers with avid interest, and found the news more cheering as the tide of war seemed to be turning in our favour. The murderous U-boats had been pounded out of the seas, bringing to an end the slaughter of our brave merchant men, who never seemed to get the credit that they deserved. In all, 36,000 Brits died in the war at sea; a telling memorial to them is the unforgettable book by Nicholas Monseratt, *The Cruel Sea*, which everyone should read who wishes to know what they had to endure.

On 6 June that year, the long-awaited assault on Europe began. A mighty armada of ships full of men and equipment crossed the Channel in choppy seas, under grey skies. Top-secret preparations had gone on for months in the south of England, but only the three war leaders knew when the signal would be given. Weather conditions in the Channel that day were not good, but they improved enough for General Dwight D. Eisenhower to say the words, 'Right, let's go'. The Germans knew that invasion was imminent, but not where or when. The Allies had chosen Normandy, and there D-Day began with sea-sick troops landing on the beaches in their thousands, everybody praying that 'Operation Overlord' would not turn to disaster like the assault on Dieppe in 1942, when thousands of Canadians died. Lists of 'killed in action', 'missing, believed killed' and 'wounded' began to appear in the papers, and the sombre voice of the newsreader on the wireless was listened to with rapt attention as each bulletin was broadcast.

While all this was going on, in Northern Italy fierce fighting continued, often in atrocious conditions. Rome was taken, then after a short respite the troops moved on towards the harsh mountain regions. With D-Day having taken over the news headlines, the troops in Italy had become the forgotten army, and bitterly they made up their own campaign song which they sang to the tune of the ever-popular 'Lili Marlene':

'We're the D-Day Dodgers, out in Italy,
Always drinking vino, always on the spree.
Eighth Army skivers and their tanks,
We live in Rome among the Yanks,
For we're the D-Day Dodgers, in sunny Italy.
Looking round the mountains in the mud and rain,
There are lots of little crosses, some which bear no name,
Blood, tears, sweat and toil are gone,
The boys beneath them slumber on,
These are your D-Day Dodgers,
Who'll stay in Italy!'

Our army was chasing the Japanese out of Burma, and thousands of GI's were clearing the Japanese from the islands in the Far East. The fighting was fierce and costly. There was still a blanket of silence over the fate of prisoners of war incarcerated by Japan after the fall of Singapore in 1942; the unfolding of that dreadful truth was yet to come. Prisoners of war in Germany following Dunkirk fared a little better. At least letters and Red Cross parcels reached them as they spent the rest of the war in the Stalags.

The Red Cross, Salvation Army, WVS and other war-relief institutions did excellent and important work in aiding morale by supplying tea, buns and biscuits to war-weary members of the armed forces. Knitting bees gathered in each others' homes, making socks, gloves, scarves and other clothing for the troops. Larger groups sat in village halls and church halls making up Red Cross parcels. At home, we bought National Savings Stamps from the lady who called at our house each week. They cost 6d. each, and we stuck them on a card provided, cashing them only when absolutely necessary. Everyone, it seemed, had a hand in the struggle, and it gave a sense of purpose to life during these long years.

That July, I travelled South again on the train to visit my parents-in-law. I liked their many village shops – baker, ironmonger, Post Office. etc

– while in the small market town of Wishaw nearby there were three cinemas and some shops, but no Woolworth's or other department store. I found the people in the village very friendly. In this small community, everybody knew everybody else, and they knew who I was. People would ask me how Bill was faring, and this was very heartwarming to me.

I picked blackcurrants from the bushes on the smallholding, and as I quickly filled the baskets it put me in mind of berry-picking in pre-war days at Hazlehead. In the Summer sunshine it was all very pleasant. I only once attempted to feed the hens in their small cages. They had a habit of pecking the hand that fed them, which I didn't like at all, even though I felt sorry for the poor things, shut away like that. My mother-in-law kept a cow named Molly, and when milking time came she would go out and call 'Moll-ee!' in a high-pitched tone. The cow would then come up from the field to the shed. One day I was left on my own while Mrs Kilgour went to the shops. To my dismay I saw Molly come through the gate, which had swung open, and begin eating the flowers and vegetables in the front garden. There I was, pleading with this cow to stop what she was doing, but she only looked at me with her limpid brown eyes and continued eating. Eventually, after gentle prodding with a stick I persuaded her to return to the field, and thankfully closed the gate behind her.

At Kaimhill, 1944

103

My country-bred mother-in-law thought it strange that I should be frightened by a cow, but that was nothing compared to what she thought the morning when I skimmed some cream from the top of a large basin of milk in the pantry and put it on my porridge. Apparently that cream was being left to form for churning into a pat of butter! Bill and I had such different backgrounds, he from the country and I from a sea-faring family. I could never have lived in a place which was forty or so miles from the coast. Even at Kaimhill, more or less on the edge of the countryside, the banks of the Dee were only a short walk away, and a tram ride would take us to the river Don.

Shortly after D-Day a letter arrived, so poignant that we wept when we read it. It was from the mother of David Wilson, the young soldier who had visited us so often with his pal. At just nineteen years of age, David had been killed in the Normandy landings, while that same week his brother-in-law died in action in Italy . David's distraught mother ended her letter by thanking our family for being so good to her son during his time of training in Aberdeen; it had, she told us, been a great comfort to know that he had such friends in his first months away from home.

I was also to remember with sadness the Hogmanay of 1939 when with my chum and two local lads, Bill Cooper and Frank Mitchell, I had first-footed my Aunt Daisy in Torry, and we had all gone to the Majestic the following night. Bill had joined the Navy and Frank the Army; Bill survived the war, but Frank died of wounds in the D-Day onslaught. He was such a nice lad, the youngest of a large family, and his eldest brother was killed in the first World War.

A request came from Wullie Young's parents – would we visit a wounded friend of theirs in the Royal Infirmary at Foresterhill? My sister and I went to see him in Ward 11, in which were several other ill and wounded soldiers, and he welcomed us warmly. His name was Rifleman Winning, and he had a wife from Yorkshire. Other soldiers in the ward who were up and about gave the good-natured 'pinkies' (staff nurses, so called because of the deep pink of their uniform) a hard time with their banter. Free from the strict army routine and (more importantly) away, at least temporarily, from the heavy fighting in Europe, they could hardly be blamed for being in high spirits, but for our Rifleman the war was over. He had lost a leg fighting in Normandy, and would now be incapacitated for the rest of his life.

As mentioned earlier, the capitulation of France in 1940 and the declaring of Paris as an open city where not a shot was fired occasioned deep anger. In those darkest times when Britain really did stand alone, stories of life in Paris sounded like heaven on earth to the inhabitants of our bomb-scarred cities. However, certain of the French, hating 'The Boche' who had taken their homeland, formed the highly effective Résistance to make the invaders' lives as difficult as possible. Many of its members were caught and executed by the German SS, but nothing could stop its continual campaign of harrassment. Wireless sets were taken out from deep in their hiding places to listen to the news on the BBC short-wave World Service, heralded always by its dash-dash-dash-dot, V-for-Victory message, the first two bars of Beethoven's Fifth Symphony. In this way, these brave people heard in late August 1944 of the Allied advance to liberate France.

In an attempt to shorten the war, the Airborne Divisions dropped thousands of parachute troops on Arnhem, Holland, in an operation named 'Market Garden'. It proved a disaster. The cost in lives was dreadful, and when we read the grim news in our newspapers we wondered, 'Will the end never come?' That September we read in the papers of the loss, in a plane over the English Channel, of the bandleader Glenn Miller, whose music had done so much to help make the war years bearable. Few can have guessed that in more than half a century's time, people would still be buying his records.

Over the remainder of 1944, thousands of men and millions of tons of guns moved across Europe in the fight to cross the Rhine. At home, the approaching winter, with fuel rationing, clothes rationed at only 24 coupons for 6 months, and butcher meat at 2s. 4d. worth per person each week, seemed likely to be a grim one, but the news was good and cheering. It was sometimes very sad as well, with its casualty and missing lists; all those grieving relatives, left with only photos and memories of their loved ones. We had been through it all before at Dunkirk and during the long desert campaign after El Alamein, our very first great victory, after which Winston Churchill had allowed the church bells to be rung. Would those bells ring out again soon, when Germany was defeated? We hoped and prayed for that.

Another parcel arrived from Bill in Italy. It contained a beautiful white fur coat and hat for our little daughter, and dresses in lovely warm material for her and Wilma. Elizabeth's photo was taken in this outfit, to which I added white velvet pants and white buckskin boots, using up precious coupons. The parcel also contained another couple of pairs of real silk stockings with seams and contoured heels. Sheer luxury. Nylon will never replace the comfort and elegance of pure silk. Bill had the sizes right, too – in fact, he had kept a note of our daughter's progress, and of course I had sent plenty of photos.

At the start of the war we sang silly songs or morale-boosting songs of defiance, but now the hits of the day were more soulful – 'I'll Be Seeing You' and 'That Lovely Weekend' – as people longed for peace and happy reunions. Undoubtedly the song of the war was 'Lili Marlene', a song full of longing for home which Allied troops first heard on the German forces' wavelengths in the desert and very quickly adopted. Although the English lyrics with which it was fitted lost rather in translation, it was heard in every sphere of the war and is still well known. Many singers sang it, but Vera Lynn gave its haunting melody a very special pathos.

The largest-scale air, sea and land assault in our history rolled across the Rhine and into Germany during the first part of 1945, with carnage on both sides. German cities were smashed to rubble by the American and British bombers. Dresden was laid waste to allow Stalin easier access from the East while the vast American armies fought from the West towards Berlin. The last German rockets were fired at this country on 27 March, after which their launching bases were reached and destroyed. It seems unbelievable now that we could watch with so little emotion as cinema newsreels brought terrible pictures of war, but since 1939 this country had been fighting for its life. All we wanted was an end to the conflict, and 1945 at last brought that hope.

In the spring of 1945 (12 April, to be exact) the papers were full of the sad news of President Franklin D. Roosevelt's death. The three-times elected President had been in poor health, but had attended meetings with Churchill and Stalin. Now it fell to his successor Harry S. Truman to lead the American nation into the post-war era.

On 28 April came the beginning of the end. That day, Mussolini was shot and killed by a communist partisan. Two days later, in his bunker below Berlin, Hitler married his long-time mistress Eva Braun, then shot her before turning the gun on himself. Banner headlines brought the news to a jubilant world, but Hitler's successor Admiral Doenitz declared that Germany would fight on, so the bitter struggle for Berlin continued, the Russians determined to gain supremacy over the British and Americans.

It lasted only a few days. Germany was finished, and on 7 May 1945 at General Eisenhower's headquarters the surrender to the Allied powers was signed. Winston Churchill proclaimed the following day VE (Victory in Europe) Day, and the nation celebrated. The church bells rang out, and at last the lights came on again after these long years of blackout, sorrow and anxiety, although out East the war was not yet over – there was still Japan.

I thought of the young men, little more than boys, that I had known who had died in the conflict, and I shed a tear for them on VE day – young men like the home-loving Joe Lamont, so handsome in his RAF uniform. A young life gone, along with the rest of the brave crew, in the debris of a plane. But horrifying news was reaching us from Germany, where our troops were coming face to face with the madman Hitler's 'final solution' in all its hellishness, and as the facts came to light we knew that we had indeed been fighting a war for good over evil.

My social life continued. One fine Sunday morning at this time, I went swimming at the beach with another girl and two young lads who were staying with us for a week's holiday. Aged eighteen, they would now at least escape war service if not a call-up for National Service. As I recall it, they came from Coatbridge via friends-of-friends of the Young family. In company with Bill's young brother and sister, who were also visiting (our good neighbour Mrs Wilson providing accommodation for the overflow) we went dancing at the Duthie Park. It was all very carefree, but there was still something missing as far as I was concerned. Then at breakfast time one morning at the end of July I opened a letter from Bill, and the words seemed to jump right out of the page at me – he was coming home! He was to travel overland from Italy on a month's LEAP leave. 'Leave, Europe Army Personnel' was its full title, I think, but I wasn't too concerned about what it was called. In all the time since we married in January 1942 we had spent only 21 days together. Would he have changed much? I was the mother of a two and half year-old child and Bill had been through all the horrors of war in the Western Desert, but it was with happy anticipation that I went to look for my least shabby clothes, my mind full of nothing but our much longed-for meeting.

Clothing coupons were so scarce that a year's allocation did not allow any extravagance, so it was very much a case of 'make do and mend'. I had two dresses made from the famous Grandholm material which never seemed to wear out. During our time at Woodside, a girl that we knew who worked in the mill had obtained the material for me, and my mother had made it into dresses. They were now four years old, but with a careful wash and press, and a touch of lace trim at the neck, they still looked good. A telegram arrived from Folkestone to say that Bill would be arriving the next day. Intending to meet him off the train in the morning, I had just removed the Dinkie curlers from my hair when I heard a familiar knock at the front door and saw the key, on its length of string behind the door, being drawn through the letter box. And there, after all this time, was the khaki-clad figure of my husband!

Leaving his kit bag on the front step, he stepped into the hallway just as our little daughter came in to stand beside me – a deeply moving moment that I will never forget. My father, who had been making breakfast, came with tears in his eyes to greet Bill. The rest of the family including my grandmother and Aunt Daisy followed suit, and suddenly the house was full of happy people, shaking hands and showering hugs and kisses on our hero who had returned from the war, even if for just a month initially. Little Elizabeth shyed away from his embrace at first, those large brown eyes looking apprehensively at this man in khaki who looked so overcome at seeing her. Spoiled by my brothers, especially my eldest brother James, it would be a little time before she responded to him.

In honour of Bill's return, we held a celebratory party, with all our friends and relatives present, and everyone contributing some food. Bill's accordion, stored away in a cupboard for so long, was brought lovingly from its case once again, and the evening sped by. Soon it was time for Bill to go and see his own folks. We visited Wull's parents, who were overjoyed when he too appeared home on LEAP leave. They gave Bill a great welcome, knowing the camaraderie that there had been between the lads since their call-up away back in 1939 – two good mates who had gone through so much together.

On his parents' smallholding, Bill assisted with the many chores just as he had done on his previous leaves from the army. He told me of how he had helped his father to build the henhouses and other outhouses when the family moved in, working day and night, and then, still just a lad, gone out to work as well. He was no stranger to 'hard graft', as he put it. When the time for parting came at the end of his leave, Bill promised that we would have a proper honeymoon when he came home again in six months, just the two of us, although it was in fact to be many years before we managed any such thing!

On 8 August, during the time that Bill was home on leave, VJ Day came. The atom bombs on Japan had finally brought to an end this terrible war. Bill was able to board his train, beginning the long journey back to Italy, in the knowledge that demob was not far off. Soon, as a dreadful addition to the story of the Nazi Holocaust, the surviving prisoners of war in Japan, these poor emaciated men, would bring back tales of atrocities. Aunt Daisy's sister-in-law and her family, imprisoned in St Thomas University for four years after the fall of Manila, while her husband was kept in another prison camp, came home telling of the horrors that they had endured. Colonials who had lived in luxury before the fall of Singapore had suddenly found themselves having to bow to the Japs for a bowl of rice. With no medical supplies to keep them, they had suffered cruelly, many of them dying of diseases like Beri-Beri. We also heard about the Burma Death Railway, of which it was said that every sleeper had cost the life of a POW. These things still cast a long shadow even after 50 years.

But on the home front it was all joy. I remember seeing long queues outside a dry cleaners' shop at the top of Union Street. Young women were standing patiently with their husbands' civvy suits, waiting to have them made ready for a serviceman's long-awaited return. It was such a happy sight. When at last Bill's final 6 month tour of duty passed, I took my daughter to the station to meet him, and my story ends with a happy scene on the station platform that day. Elizabeth knew her Daddy even though he was still in uniform, and he received his full share of hugs and kisses from both of us. Outside our house in Kaimhill, (and outside many others at this time), flags and buntings fluttered in the cold wind. A large placard proclaimed 'Welcome Home, Bill'. No more partings, and no more the heartbreak and stress of long separations. No more Hitler, no more Luftwaffe, and no more dread of receiving War Office telegrams. In 1940 this little island had stood alone against the armed might of Germany – 'our finest hour', Winston Churchill had called it. Against all odds, we had won the war; would we now win the peace? Only time would tell.

I am proud to be of a generation that endured so much over those six long, hard years – a generation that fought and died for a country that had offered it so pitifully little during the previous decade. It is said that war is a breakdown of civilisation, but with the Nazi regime civilisation did not exist, and this was a just battle which had to be fought, even though it cost millions of lives. I fervently hope that the horrors of war will never touch the young generation of today, and that young people will know that but for the sacrifices of their forebears this world would have sunk into the abyss of a new and unimaginably savage dark age.

Walking hand-in-hand into the sunset sounds like the typical popular happy ending to any story. Thoughts of what the future held for us did not stay long in our minds, so happy were we and the thousands of other young couples re-united after long separation.

We were survivors of a long and bitter war, now we could look forward to the Brave New World and the fruits of victory.

Austerity, continued rationing of food and clothing was nothing compared to the hardship of having no home of our own even in the near future. We lived in crowded parental households, while endeavouring to get to know each other, having spent so little time together during leaves from the Army.

Many war-time weddings succumbed to the pressures, ending in divorce, but for the majority who, in the face of all adversity, saw at last a light at the end of the tunnel, there was to be a post war world of peace.